Tipbook
Acoustic Guitar

The Complete Guide

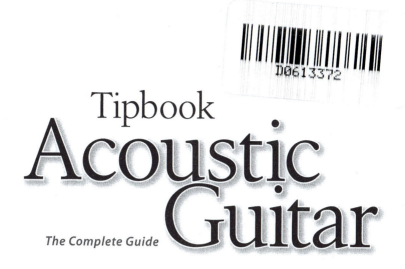

Hugo Pinksterboer

Tipbook
Acoustic
Guitar

The Complete Guide

HAL•LEONARD®

The Complete Guide to Your Instrument!

First edition published in 2002 by The Tipbook Company bv,
The Netherlands

Second edition published in 2008 by
Hal Leonard Books
An Imprint of Hal Leonard Corporation
7777 West Bluemound Road
Milwaukee, WI 53213

Trade Book Division Editorial Offices
19 West 21st Street, New York, NY 10010

Printed in the United States

Book design by Gijs Bierenbroodspot

Library of Congress Cataloging-in-Publication Data

Pinksterboer, Hugo.
Tipbook acoustic guitar : the complete guide /
Hugo Pinksterboer. — 2nd ed.
    p. cm.
Includes bibliographical references and index.
ISBN 978-1-4234-4275-2
1. Guitar. I. Title.
ML1015.G9P546 2008
787.87'19—dc22

                            2008044527

www.halleonard.com

Thanks!

For their information, their expertise, their time, and their help we'd like to thank the following musicians, teachers, technicians, and other guitar experts:

Harry Sacksioni, Erik Vaarzon Morel, Olaf Tarenskeen, the late Willy Heijnen (*Meet Music Magazine*), Ulbo de Sitter, Arno van den Wijngaard (Feedback), Harm van der Geest, Frans van Ingen (*Music Maker*), Corrie de Haan, Nicky Moeken (*Gitaar Plus*), Ron Houben (Houben Guitars), Chris Teerlink and Martin van der Lucht, Gilbert Maurice Herngreen, Harry de Jonge (Sacksioni Guitars), Henny van Ochten (Texas & Tweed), Nils Rurack, Michel de Groot, Jan Verweij, Jean Zijta, and Lex Horst.

We also wish to thank Teja Gerken (*Acoustic Guitar magazine*) for his last-minute assistance, Elliot Freedman for his valuable input, Nahim Avci (Rotterdam Conservatory), Roy op de Kamp (Papen & Bongaerts), Harold Koenders (JIC), Ivar Lelieveld (Muziekhandel Dijkman), Ben van der Sman (Casa Benelly), Niek Stoop, Rick Verhoeff (BMI), and Bart Witte (Dirk Witte Muziek).

Special thanks go to guitarist and writer John van der Veer for being a valuable and ever-present source of information, to editor and guitarist Michiel Roelse (*Gitarist*) for his contributions to the book, and to Gerard Braun for his musical help in making the Tipcode-videos and creating the chord diagram section.

J. Hayes, thanks for your support — again!

About the Author

Journalist and musician **Hugo Pinksterboer**, author and editor of The Tipbook Series has published hundreds of interviews, articles and instrument reviews, and DVD, CD, and book reviews for a variety of international music magazines.

About the Designer

Illustrator, designer, and musician **Gijs Bierenbroodspot** has worked as an art director for a wide variety of magazines and has developed numerous ad campaigns. While searching in vain for information about saxophone mouthpieces, he got the idea for this series of books on music and musical instruments. He is responsible for the layout and illustrations of all of the Tipbooks.

Acknowledgments

Cover photo: René Vervloet
Editors: Robert L. Doerschuk, Michael J. Collins, and Meg Clark
Proofreaders: Nancy Bishop and Patricia Waddy

Anything missing?

Any omissions? Any areas that could be improved? Please go to www.tipbook.com to contact us. Thanks!

Contents

VII

Introduction

Do you plan to buy an acoustic guitar or acoustic bass guitar, or do you want to learn more about the one you already have? If so, this book will tell you all you need to know. You'll learn about the parts of the instrument and what they do; lessons and practicing; auditioning and testing guitars; pickups, strings, picks, and straps; tuning and maintenance; the instrument's history and family — and much more.

Having read this Tipbook, you'll be able to get the most out of your instrument, to buy the best acoustic guitar you can, and to easily grasp any other literature on the subject, from books and magazines to online publications.

The best you can
Having read this Tipbook, you'll be able to get the most out of your instrument, to buy the best acoustic guitar you can, and to easily grasp any other literature on the subject, from books and magazines to online publications.

The first four chapters
If you have just started playing, or haven't yet begun, pay particular attention to the first four chapters. They explain the basics of the instrument, and they inform you on learning to play, practicing, and buying or renting an acoustic guitar. The information in these chapters also fully prepares you to read the rest of the book.

X

Advanced players

Advanced players can skip ahead to Chapter 5, where you will find everything you need to know to make an informed choice when you're going to buy a guitar, introducing you to the effects of different types of woods, and to finishes, body sizes, neck profiles, scales, frets, and more. Chapter 6 offers similar information on acoustic-electric guitars, and chapter 7 helps you find the right strings for your instrument.

Maintenance and more

The following chapters are dedicated to instrument maintenance and making your instrument sound good, with helpful and practical information on changing and cleaning strings, selecting picks, nail care, and tuning your guitar — including tips for advanced players!

Background information

The final four chapters offer information on the history, the family, the production and the makers of the instrument.

Street prices

Please note that all prices mentioned in this book are based on estimated street prices in US dollars.

And more

The glossary and index turn this book into a handy reference, and information on additional resources on the instrument can be found on pages 179–182. As another extra, the book provides two pages for essential notes on your equipment.

Chord diagrams

Many readers of earlier editions of this Tipbook asked us to include guitar and bass chord diagrams— and so we did. This information is also available online, but a book is easier to take along (and you don't have to turn it on either). So here they are. Enjoy!

— Hugo Pinksterboer

XI

See and Hear What You Read with Tipcodes

www.tipbook.com

In addition to the many illustrations on the following pages, Tipbooks offer you an another way to see — and even hear — what you are reading about. The Tipcodes that you will come across regularly in this book give you access to extra pictures, short videos, sound files, and other additional information at www.tipbook.com.

Here's how it works. Below the *Tip* on fingerpicking on page 45 is a short section marked **Tipcode AGTR-005**. Type in that code on the Tipcode page at www.tipbook.com and you will see a short video that demonstrates the particular playing technique. Similar videos are available on a variety of subjects; other Tipcodes will link to a sound file.

TIPCODE

Tipcode AGTR-005
Fingerpicking guitarists play both a bass line and the melody.

Repeat

If you miss something the first time, you can of course replay the Tipcode. And if it all happens too fast, use the pause button beneath the movie window.

Tipcode list

For your convenience, the Tipcodes presented in this book are listed on page 178.

Plug-ins

If the software you need to view the videos is not yet installed on your computer, you'll automatically be told which software you

First, make your selection: Tipcode, chords and fingering charts, or the glossary.

The Tipcode window displays movies, photo series, fingering charts, chords, and explanations of the words used in this book.

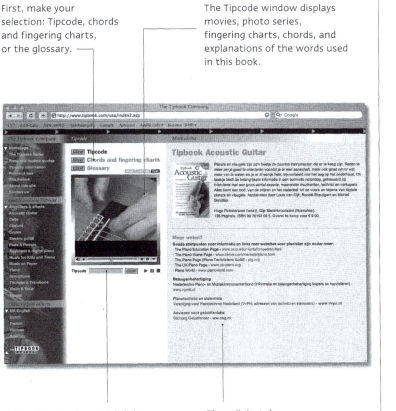

Enter a Tipcode here and click on the button. Want to see it again? Click again.

These links take you directly to other interesting sites.

XIII

need, and where you can download it. This type of software is
free. Questions? Check out 'About this site' at www.tipbook.com.

Still more at www.tipbook.com

You can find even more information at www.tipbook.com.
For instance, you can look up words in the glossaries of all the
Tipbooks published to date. There are chord diagrams
for guitarists and pianists; fingering charts for saxophonists,
clarinetists, and flutists; and rudiments for drummers. Also
included are links to most of the websites mentioned in the *Want
to Know More?* section of each Tipbook.

1. A Guitarist?

As a guitarist, you can play a handful of chords to accompany a song, or a virtuoso solo over the solid foundation of a four-piece rock band. You can also play a classical concert, alone or with a full-sized orchestra, or accompany a dance group or a choir. From campfire to stadium concert, from nightclub to living room, acoustic guitarists can play anywhere — and there are almost as many different guitars as there are guitarists.

The guitar is one of the instruments that allows you to play *chords* (three or more notes simultaneously), which adds a lot to its versatility. When you can play chords, you don't need the accompaniment of a band, so you can play music all by yourself — but you can also play simple melodies or intricate solos.

Acoustic or electric

You can do so with an electric guitar too, of course. So what's the main difference between acoustic and electric guitars, other than the sound?

- Acoustic guitars have a large **soundbox** that acoustically 'amplifies' the sound of your strings.

- Most electric guitars have a **solid body** instead of a soundbox, which explains why you need an amp to play the instrument.

Steel or nylon

There are two main types of acoustic guitars: the steel-string guitar and the classical, nylon-string guitar.

Classical, Spanish, or nylon-string

The *classical guitar* is mainly — but not only! — used for classical guitar music. The instrument has nylon strings. It is also known as the *Spanish guitar*, as that was the country where it was given its final form.

Classical or Spanish nylon-string guitar.

Steel-string guitar, western guitar, folk guitar

Steel-string guitars originally come from the US. The names *western guitar* and *folk guitar* are also often used. Steel-string guitars sound a bit louder and brighter than classical guitars.

Steel-string, western guitar, or folk guitar.

Even more

There are many more types of acoustic guitars — twelve-string guitars, for example, or resonator guitars (with one or more metal resonators), acoustic bass guitars with four or five strings, and acoustic-electric guitars, which you can hook up to an amplifier, just like an electric guitar.

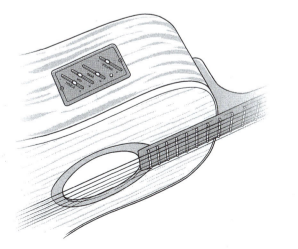

An electric-acoustic guitar can be hooked up to an amplifier. The controls of the guitar are usually located on the upper bout.

3

Their own sound
All these different guitars have a sound or *timbre* of their own. Many have a sound that suits a certain style of music, like the flamenco guitar or the jazz guitar, or a certain way of playing, like the twelve-string guitar, with it characteristic, ringing tone.

Singer-songwriter
One of the fun things about the guitar is that you need no more than a couple of guitar chords to play hundreds of songs in a wide variety of styles. It will usually take you little time to learn how to accompany a singer, for example — and that singer could very well be you. Most Singer-songwriters are guitarists, and many of them perform solo.

Strumming or plucking
Instead of playing chords (*strumming*), you can also pluck the strings with your fingers and nails. This allows you to play a bass line with your thumb, and the melody with your other fingers, for example. Classical guitarists basically play this way, and so do fingerpickers (see page 45).

Sitting down
You can play the instrument standing up or sitting down. When seated, steel-string guitarists typically rest the guitar's body on their right thigh. Classical guitarists put it on their left upper leg, using either a pillow or a guitar support on their leg to lift the instrument a little. A foot rest under the left foot has the same

TIPCODE

Tipcode AGTR-001
Classical guitarist, playing a bass line and the melody at the same time.

4

effect, but it makes you twist your body, possibly causing back aches and other symptoms.

Picks or nails

Steel-string guitars are usually played with a pick, while classical guitarists use their fingertips or their nails to pluck their nylon-stringed instruments. This stresses the difference in sound between steel-string and nylon-string guitars.

Not just classical music

Classical guitarists use nylon-string guitars — but you can use this instrument for many other styles of music too, ranging from pop and latin to jazz, for example. Some companies make special types of nylon-stringed instruments for those styles, including guitars that can be used with synthesizers and other digital equipment (see page 157).

TIP

Popular instrument

The acoustic guitar is one of the world's most popular instruments. Here's why.

- They're very affordable. **It won't cost you much money** to buy yourself a guitar you can enjoy for years to come — although you can just as easily spend a couple of months' wages on one.

- The guitar is **not difficult** to learn. That doesn't mean you'll soon be finished learning either; in the end, the guitar is as hard to master as the piano, the drums, or any other instrument.

- A guitar weighs next to nothing, so you can easily take it along wherever you go.

- Acoustic guitars aren't loud enough to annoy your neighbors, but there's **no need for an amplifier** to hear what you're playing.

Acoustic or electric

Many guitarists play both acoustic and electric instruments, usually starting out on an acoustic one and switching to an

5

electric guitar after a couple of years. That's a great way to learn the instrument. The acoustic guitar typically demands some extra dedication and practice to make it sound good, and bringing that experience to the electric guitar will make you sound even better. On the other hand, you can of course start playing on an electric instrument and add an acoustic guitar to your collection later on, as many players do.

2

A Quick Tour

Seen from a distance, an acoustic guitar seems to be nothing more than a body in the shape of a huge figure-8, and a neck. When you get closer, there's a lot more to see. An introduction to the main parts of the instrument, starting with the classical guitar, then the steel-string guitar, and finally the acoustic-electric guitar.

One look at the *head* on the instrument will usually tell you whether you're dealing with a classical or a steel-string guitar. If it is slotted, you're probably looking at a classical, nylon-string guitar. Most steel-string instruments have a solid head. Heads are also referred to as *headstocks* or *pegheads*.

The slotted head of a classical guitar, and the solid head of a steel-string guitar.

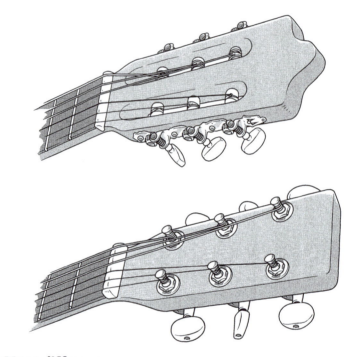

More differences

Three more differences:

• Steel-string models usually have **larger bodies** and narrower necks.

• They often have a **pickguard** to protect the body against scratches by picks and nails.

• You can clearly see that the three thinnest strings are made of **steel**, rather than of nylon.

The sound

Classical guitars also have a different sound, mainly because of their strings. They sound warmer, mellower or 'drier' than steel-

8

string guitars, which sound brighter and — of course — more metallic. The sound of steel-strings also projects better.

Tipcode AGTR-002
This Tipcode demonstrates the different timbres of steel-string and nylon-string guitars.

TIPCODE

TIP

Nylon or steel?

For classical music, you should of course get a classical guitar. Learning to play chords is easier with the narrower neck of a steel-string. Steel-strings may be a little more uncomfortable in the beginning, however. Switching to light gauge strings helps!

CLASSICAL GUITARS

If you look only at all the main parts and what they do, a classical guitar is very similar to a steel-string instrument.

The top
The wood of the body's *top* is very important for the sound of every guitar, as you can tell from its second name — *soundboard*. The left side of the top is often the exact mirror image of the right side; if so, it's a *bookmatched* top.

Back and sides
Between top and *back* are the *sides* or *rims*.

9

Soundhole and rosette

When you take a look inside, there's usually a label bearing the name and logo of the manufacturer, or the name and signature of the guitar maker or *luthier*. The decoration around the *soundhole* is called the *rosette*.

Binding

The *bindings* protect and finish the edges of the body. Some guitars also have bindings around the head and the neck.

Waist, lower bout and upper bout

The wider parts of the body are called the *upper bout* and the *lower bout* or *belly*. In between is the *waist*.

Heel

The *heel* is the wooden block at the point where the neck is attached to the body.

Fingerboard

The strings run along the *fingerboard*, onto which you press your fingers to *stop* the strings. Stopping a string shortens the section of the string that vibrates, thus producing a higher pitch.

Frets

The small metal strips on the fingerboard are the *frets*. They make a guitar easier to play in tune than a violin or a cello, for example. These bowed instruments have no frets.

Fretboard

Because of the frets, the fingerboard is also known as *fretboard*. 'Playing the fourth fret' means pressing the string just behind the fourth fret. Stopping a string is also known as *fretting* a string.

TIP

The twelfth fret

You don't need position markers to find the twelfth fret: It's the fret where the body meets the neck. Stopping a string at this fret makes it sound an octave higher.

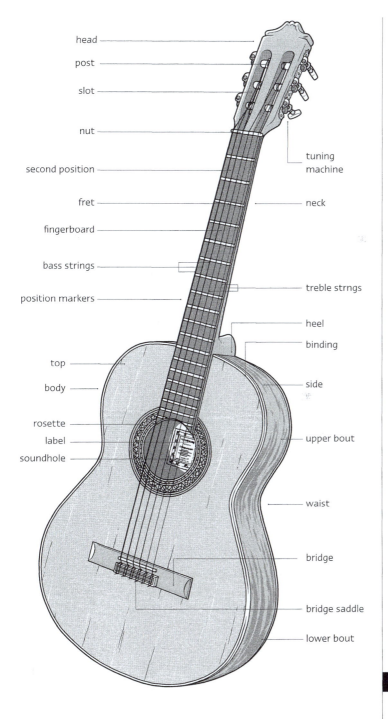

head

post

slot

nut

second position

fret

fingerboard

bass strings

position markers

top

body

rosette

label

soundhole

tuning machine

neck

treble strngs

heel

binding

side

upper bout

waist

bridge

bridge saddle

lower bout

Position markers

On the upper side of the fingerboard you may find a series of *position markers* or *markers* — small dots that indicate the fret or the *position* you're at.

Posts and tuners

The strings are wound around the *string posts*. You tune the guitar with the *tuning machines* or *tuners*, either tightening or loosening the strings.

Strings

The thinnest, highest-sounding string is called the *first string*. The thickest string, or the *sixth string*, sounds the lowest. As a reminder: The thinnest string has the 'thinnest' number, 1. The thickest string has a thick-looking number, the 6.

E, A, D, G, B, E

The six strings, from thick to thin, low to high, are tuned to the notes E, A, D, G, B, E. These pitches can be easily memorized as Eating And Drinking Give Brain Energy; two more memory aids can be found in Chapter 9.

TIP

Numbered octaves

A guitar has two E-strings. Low E sounds two octaves lower than high E. To avoid confusion between higher and lower notes with the same note name, they have been numbered.

- Low E on a guitar sounds the same pitch as the 2nd lowest E on a piano. It's known as E2.

- High E on a guitar sounds the same pitch as the 4th E on a piano keyboard (counting from the left), so it's referred to as E4.

- Adding these numbers to the notes, the strings of a guitar are tuned to the following pitches: E2, A2, D3, G3, B3, E4.

12

Wound strings

You can easily see that the thin strings are made of nylon. The three thickest ones are nylon too, but they look quite different because they're wound with metal wire. Their name is obvious: *wound strings*.

Bass and treble

These wound strings are also known as the *bass strings*. The non-wound or *plain strings* are also known as the *treble strings* or *melody strings*.

Nut

Between the head and the neck, the strings run over the *nut*. The not or *top nut* makes sure that the strings run at the right height over the neck. The slots or notches in the nut make sure they do so at equal distances from each other.

Bridge and saddle

At the other end, the strings tie around the *bridge*. The light-colored strip on the bridge that supports the strings is called the *bridge saddle*.

Confusing

Some guitarists use the term 'bridge' to refer to either the saddle or the nut, which can be confusing.

STEEL-STRING GUITARS

Steel-string guitars come in many different sizes and shapes, of which the Jumbo and the Dreadnought are the two biggest. Chapters 5 and 13 tell you more about those sizes. The names of the main parts of the guitar, from body to headstock, have been mentioned above.

Pickguard

The pickguard protects the top from nails and picks, which may otherwise scratch it when strumming chords.

13

Bindings
The bindings of steel-string instruments often have special patterns (e.g., herringbone).

The fourteenth fret
The body usually starts at the fourteenth fret instead of the twelfth, as on classical guitars. To use the lingo: most steel-string guitars have a *fourteen-fret neck*.

Cutaway
Some steel-string guitars also have a *cutaway*, giving easier access to the highest positions on the neck. You'll find two examples on pages 47–48.

Markers
Most steel-string guitars have *position markers* on the side of the neck and on the fingerboard. The twelfth fret, where strings sound an octave higher than playing them open, often has a larger or a different marking.

An octave on a steel-string guitar neck.

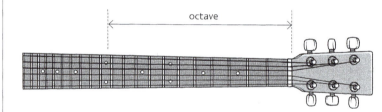

octave

Plain and wound strings
Most steel-string guitars have two thin *plain strings* and four thicker *wound strings*. Their standard tuning is identical to that of a nylon-string guitar: E, A, D, G, B, E (see page 12).

A narrower neck
The neck of a steel-string guitar is narrower than that of a classical guitar, making it easier to finger chords.

Camber
If you look along the neck from the headstock you'll see that the fingerboard is slightly curved. It's a bit higher underneath the

14

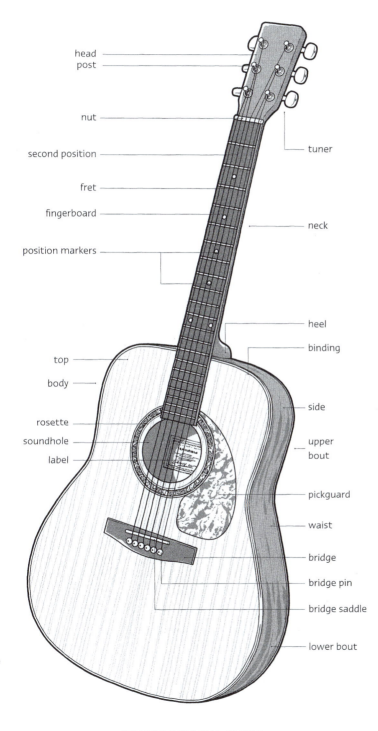

head
post

nut

second position

fret

fingerboard

position markers

top
body

rosette
soundhole
label

tuner

neck

heel
binding

side

upper
bout

pickguard

waist

bridge

bridge pin

bridge saddle

lower bout

middle strings, with a very slight downward slope toward the outer strings. This curvature is known as the fingerboard *radius* or *camber*.

Truss rod

Steel-strings pull harder than nylon strings. To counteract that extra tension, an adjustable metal *truss rod* is built into the neck.

Bridge

The bridges on most steel-string guitars have a distinctive shape, which often allows you to tell the make of the instrument.

Bridge saddle

The bridge saddle of a steel-string guitar is usually not at a right angle to the strings, and sometimes consists of two or more parts.

Bridge pins

Right behind the bridge saddle you can see the heads of the *bridge pins* which hold the strings in place. Bridge pins are also known as *pegs*. Most guitars use plastic pins, but wooden pins (ebony or boxwood, for example) are also available.

Flattops and archtops

The name *flattop* distinguishes steel-string guitars with a flat top from instruments with an arched top. *Arch-top guitars* are somewhat similar to violins, due to the arched top, the *f*-shaped soundholes, and the fact that the strings are attached to a tailpiece rather than to the bridge.

An arch-top guitar with f-shaped soundholes.

BASS GUITARS

Acoustic bass guitars are tuned to the same notes as electric bass guitars or the double bass. Their four strings sound an octave lower than the four lowest sounding strings of a guitar (E1, A1, D2, G2; see page 12).

Thicker and longer
To allow the bass guitar strings to sound these low pitches, they are about twice as thick as the corresponding guitar strings. They're also a bit longer. All bass strings are wound strings.

THE INSIDE

Classical and steel-string guitars differ on the inside as well.

Bracing
The top is reinforced by a number of braces, which also influence the sound. Most classical guitars have *fan-bracing*; seven braces, laid out in the shape of a fan. The braces against the back are called *ribs* or *struts*.

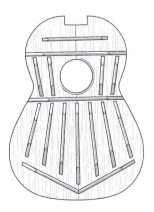 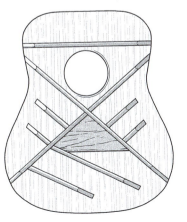

Left: the braces of a classical guitar (fan-bracing); right: the braces of a steel-string guitar (X-bracing).

17

Pattern

The braces in steel-string guitars have a different pattern. The so-called *X-bracing* is the traditional and most common type.

LEFT-HANDED

Most left-handed guitarists use 'right-handed' guitars, strumming or plucking the strings with their right hand and stopping them with the fingers of their left hand. Others prefer a left-handed guitar. Classical guitars can be adapted for left-handed playing quite easily, although it takes more than just putting the strings on the other way around.

A steel-string guitar for left-handed guitarists.

Adapting guitars

Adapting a steel-string guitar is a bit harder, if only because the pattern of the braces underneath the thick strings differs from that underneath the thin ones. If you would reverse the strings, you'd have to reverse the bracing as well, which is too much work. However, cheaper steel-string guitars are sometimes converted for left-handed use without adapting the braces, with no major consequences for the sound.

A better solution

It's usually better to simply buy a left-handed guitar. There are fewer instruments to choose from, and you may have to pay a bit extra, but it's worth it. If you prefer a guitar with a cutaway, you

18

will definitely need to get a left-handed model: If you play a right-handed guitar the other way around, the cutaway will be on the upper shoulder.

TIP

> ### The other way around
>
> *A few left-handed guitarists play a left-handed guitar with 'right-handed' strings, i.e., low E is their first string. Their major advantage is that they can play any right-handed guitar as well!*

ACOUSTIC-ELECTRIC GUITARS

If your guitar isn't loud enough, you can stick a microphone in front of it. Most guitarists, however, prefer a guitar with a built-in pickup. That way they can hook it up directly to an amplifier, just like an electric guitar. Acoustic guitars with built-in pickups are known as *acoustic-electric* (*A/E*) or *electro-acoustic guitars*. Usually these are 'regular' steel-string guitars, the only difference being the pickup and the electronics that come with it.

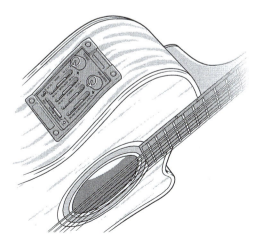

The control panel of an acoustic-electric guitar.

19

Pickup

A pickup literally 'picks up' the vibrations of the strings, translating them into electric signals that can be amplified. Most acoustic-electric guitars have *piezo pickups*, invisibly mounted under the saddle of the guitar. Chapter 6, *Acoustic-electric guitars*, tells you all about them.

Controls

Controls for volume, tone, and other parameters are usually located on the upper bout of the guitar, or in the soundhole. They operate the built-in *preamplifier* or *preamp*, which boosts the pickup signal before sending it out to the main amp.

3

Learning to Play

Is it hard to play the guitar? That depends on what you want to play. You can learn the chords to a couple of songs in a few weeks. But what if you want to play classical music, or if you want to master more than some popular chords? A chapter on chord diagrams, lessons, notes, and practicing — and on how easy it can be.

If you want to play classical guitar music, you can't get around learning to read notes. Yet many guitarists in other styles don't use traditional notation. They rely on chord diagrams or tablature, which are two different ways to put guitar music on paper.

Play string 3 at the first fret with your index finger, play string 5 at the second fret with your middle finger, and play string 4 at the second fret with your ring finger. The result is an E-major chord.

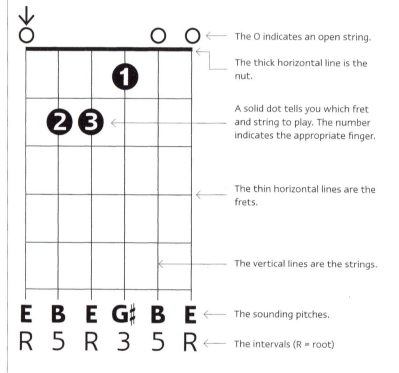

The O indicates an open string.

The thick horizontal line is the nut.

A solid dot tells you which fret and string to play. The number indicates the appropriate finger.

The thin horizontal lines are the frets.

The vertical lines are the strings.

The sounding pitches.

The intervals (R = root)

Three or four chords

Many famous songs in many popular styles of music consist of only three or four chords — from the blues and the Beatles to Metallica and Madonna. Once you learn those chords by heart and practice them for a couple of weeks, you'll be able to play plenty of tunes.

Chord diagrams

A chord diagram is a chart that shows you where to put your fingers for each different chord. This book offers you a wide variety of chord diagrams (starting on page 183), and there are dozens of dedicated books that provide even more chords.

22

Tipcode AGTR-003
This is what the blues pictured below sounds like.

The blues

Here's an example of what you can do with chord diagrams: Just learn the three chords below, and you can play a twelve-bar blues tune.

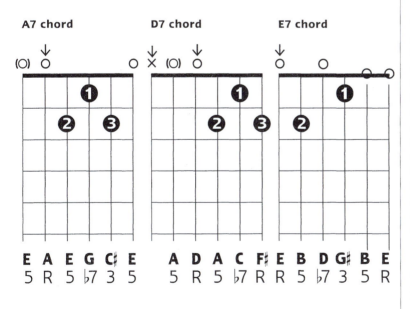

A7 chord	D7 chord	E7 chord

E	A	E	G	C♯	E		A	D	A	C	F♯	E		B	D	G♯	B	E
5	R	5	♭7	3	5		5	R	5	♭7	R	R		5	♭7	3	5	R

O = open string; must sound

(O) = open string; may sound

↓ = root note; best bass sound

X = doesn't sound; don't strike

To play a twelve-bar blues tune, all you need are these three simple chords. Each of the twelve bars consists of four beats. Play 1x (one bar, equaling four counts) A7, 1xD7, 2xA7, 2xD7, 2xA7, 1xE7, 1xD7, 1xA7 and 1xE7. Repeat this as long as you like. The last time around, you replace the E7 in the last bar by A7.

23

Tablature

Chord diagram or charts are a shortcut for reading the notes of the chords in traditional notation. There's a similar solution for guitar solos and bass lines, called *tablature* or *tabs*, shown below*. The horizontal lines represent the strings of your guitar, and numbers are used to indicate where to fret the strings and which fingers to use. Tablature doesn't allow for precise rhythmical notation, so traditional notation is often included.

The tablature staff represents a guitar neck.

The numbers of the strings.

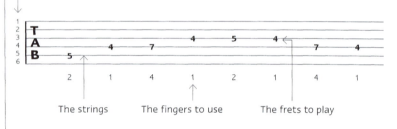

The strings   The fingers to use   The frets to play

Traditional notation

With the exception of classical players, there are thousands of guitarists who don't read traditional music notation— including some who are quite famous. However, it may not be a bad idea to learn traditional notation too, even if classical music is not your thing. Here are some reasons why.

- You'll have access to **lots of books and magazines** with exercises, songs, and solos — even when they're not in tablature.

- It'll give you a **better insight** into the way chords and songs are structured.

- It enables you to **put down on paper** your own songs, solos, ideas, and exercises.

- The ability to read music makes you **more of a musician**, instead of 'just' a guitarist.

- And finally: Learning to read music **isn't that hard at all**. *Tipbook Music on Paper — Basic Theory* teaches you the basics within a few chapters (see page 234).

LESSONS

Hardly anybody learns to play classical guitar music without taking lessons, as it's very hard to master classical guitar technique on your own. For other types of music, consulting a teacher isn't a bad idea either.

Teachers

Of course you can work out everything on your own, but why would you when there are people who can teach you. Or they can at least tell you the basics, so that you start out the right way. Again, there are plenty of famous guitarists who wouldn't know what a music teacher looks like. There are also plenty of famous guitarists who have had lessons. And quite a few of them still do, occasionally.

Learning more

Good teachers not only teach good technique, they will work on a good tone, good posture, reading music, tuning, playing different styles of music, and much more.
Classical lessons may still be a good start, even if you think you're going to end up playing something completely different.

TIP

Questions, questions

On your first visit to a teacher, don't just ask how much it costs. Here are some other questions.

• Is an **introductory lesson** included? This is a good way to find out how well you get on with the teacher, and for that matter, with the instrument.

• Is the teacher interested in taking you on as a student even if you are doing it **just for the fun of it**, or will he or she expect you to practice at least three hours a day?

25

- Will you have to make a large investment in method books right away, or is **the course material provided**?

- Can you **record your lessons**, so that you can listen again to how you sounded and what was said when you get home?

- Will you be allowed to concentrate fully on **the style of music you want to play**, or will you be required to learn other styles? Will you be stimulated to do so?

- Will this teacher make you **practice scales** for two years, or will you be encouraged to perform as soon as possible?

Finding a teacher

Looking for a private teacher? Larger music stores may have teachers on staff, or they can refer you to one, and some players have found great teachers in musicians they have seen in a performance. You can also find teachers online (see page 182). Alternatively, you may consult your local Musicians' Union, the band director at a high school in your vicinity, or check the classified ads in newspapers or music magazines. Professional private teachers will usually charge between twenty-five and seventy-five dollars per hour. Some make house calls, for which you'll pay extra.

Group or individual lessons

While most guitar students take individual lessons, you can also try group lessons if that's an option in your area. Private lessons are more expensive, but they can be tailored exactly to your needs.

Collectives

You also may want to check whether there are any teacher's collectives or music schools in your area. These collectives may offer extras such as ensemble playing, master classes, and clinics, in a wide variety of styles and at various levels.

PRACTICING

You can learn to play without reading notes, or even without a teacher. But no one ever learned to play without practicing.

How long?
How long you need to practice depends on what you want to achieve. Many great instrumentalists have practiced four to eight hours a day for years, or more. The more time you spend practicing (and playing!), the faster your playing will improve. Half an hour a day usually results in steady progress.

Shorter sessions
If you find it hard to practice half an hour a day, try dividing it up into two quarter-hour sessions, or three of ten minutes each.

TIP

Setting goals
Rather than focusing on how long you need to practice, it may be wise to set a goal for each practice session, or for the next week. That allows you to focus on the music, rather than on the clock!

Hang in there
Do note that playing the guitar will take some getting used to, at first. Especially your left hand, because it gets to do a lot of work, in a rather awkward position. On a steel-string guitar you'll also feel the strings cutting into your fingertips. Hang in there; it will pass. A *Tip*: Using lighter-gauge strings will alleviate some of the initial discomfort.

Acoustic or electric?
Playing an acoustic guitar is different from playing an electric one. It's harder to press down the strings, for one. It also takes more effort to make an acoustic guitar sound really good. This is precisely why the acoustic guitar is an excellent instrument to start

on, whether you plan to keep playing acoustically or not. Playing electric will only be made easier.

Silent guitar

You don't make a lot of sound as you practice your instrument, so in most situations you can play at any time you want. Should you still bother housemates or your neighbors, you may consider buying a silent guitar. Instead of a soundbox, these instruments have a single 'frame' that typically resembles the outline of a regular instrument. You can hear yourself play by connecting a pair of headphones to the built-in headphone amplifier. A (digital) reverb is usually on board, making the amplified sound come alive. *Tip:* As they don't have a soundbox, such guitars are extremely portable too!

Play along

Most of these instruments feature a line input. Connecting an additional sound source such as an mp3 player allows you to play along with prerecorded music. With an extra output the guitar can be hooked up to an amp (see pages 78–80), so you can use it onstage or in the studio as well.

Hearing protection

If you play your instrument in a band and there's a drummer involved, your guitar will need to be amplified. In most cases, you will then use an acoustic-electric guitar. Most bands play and practice at volumes that can cause hearing loss or hearing damage pretty easily, so do consider using some kind of hearing protection, both at rehearsals and at gigs. As hearing damage is often noticed only when it's too late, prevention is the key. Bear in mind that hearing loss is usually irreversible, and ringing ears (*tinnitus*) can keep on ringing for years.

Cheap or expensive earplugs...

The cheapest foam plastic earplugs, available from most music stores and drugstores, will make your band sound as if it's playing next door. The most expensive earplugs are custom-made to fit your ears (*otoplastics*). These plugs often have adjustable filters that reduce the volume without affecting the sound.

... and in between

Plastic earplugs come in many variations. Some just reduce the overall volume; others make the band sound dull and far away, just like earmuffs do. Also, some are easier to clean than others. Ask fellow musicians (drummers!) for their experiences with hearing protection, and don't hesitate to try different products until you find the ones that really fit and work for you. They may not come cheap, but a hearing aid costs more.

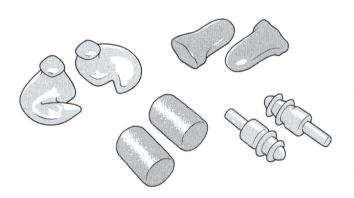

Some affordable types of ear plugs.

In-ear monitors

In-ear monitors *can also help protect your hearing. These custom made earplugs have built-in speakers, replacing the traditional — and often very loud — onstage monitor speakers. You can simply adjust the volume of your in-ear monitors so that you hear what you need to hear, and no more than that.*

TIP

Books, DVDs, CDs, CD-ROMs

Guitarists have easy access to lots of reference material.

- **Guitar books** come in all shapes and sizes, for absolute beginners and absolute pros. Quite a few of them come with one or more CDs that include examples or play-along exercises; you turn off the sound of the guitarist and play that part yourself.

- Most **guitar magazines** offer chord diagrams, tablature, and other practice materials too.

29

- **Educational guitar DVDs** are often made by well-known guitarists who show you their tricks of the trade. These video lessons usually last anywhere from thirty to ninety minutes. A booklet with printouts of the recorded rhythms and exercises is sometimes included.

- There are **CD-ROMs** that turn your computer into a guitar teacher — and there are online guitar lessons available as well.

Keeping time

You usually end a piece in the tempo you started at. So it's good to practice with a metronome, at least once in a while. A metronome is a small device that ticks or beeps out a steady, adjustable pulse, which helps you to work on your tempo, timing, and rhythm.

Two mechanical metronomes and two electronic ones.

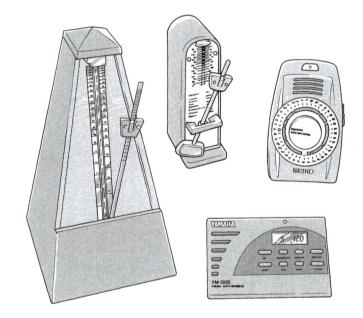

Electronics and computers

A drum machine is a great alternative to the metronome. There are similar machines that can play bass lines and other programmable instruments too, and there are machines and software programs that offer you an entire band to play along with.

30

Phrase trainers

Phrase trainers are devices that can slow down a musical phrase from a CD, for example, so you can figure out even the meanest, fastest licks at your own tempo. There is software available that does the same thing.

TIP

Record your music

No matter how good you are, it's always hard to judge you own playing as you play. Tip: record your practice sessions, or your first or subsequent attempts to play the piece that you have been practicing, and then judge your performance by listening to the recording, once or a couple of times. This is very instructive for musicians at any level. Also consider recording your lessons, so you can listen once more to what was said, and especially to how you sounded, when you get home. All you need is a portable recording device with a built-in microphone. A computer is great for home recording!

Get to work

And finally, visit festivals, concerts, and sessions. Listen to bands and soloists. One of the best ways to learn to play is through seeing other musicians at work. Living legends or local amateurs — every gig's a learning experience. And the very best way to learn to play? Play a lot!

4

Buying a Guitar

One of the nice things about guitars is that you can buy
a pretty good instrument for very little money — on
the other hand, you can just as easily spend thousands
of dollars on one. The following chapter tells you
everything you'll want to know before going out to buy
an instrument. Chapters 5 and 6 deal with what to listen
and watch out for once you're in the store.

One or two hundred dollars is all you need to buy a brand new acoustic guitar. This is very little money, when you consider that the guitar has to be made, shipped, and sold for that price. So don't expect too much — but you will at least be able to play. A top-of-the-line instrument can easily cost fifty times as much.

Solid top

Most teachers will advise you not to begin on the cheapest guitar you can buy. It's better to spend a little more on a decent instrument, preferably with a solid top (see page 49). These usually start at around two to three hundred dollars. The extra money buys you an instrument that's probably easier to tune and easier to play, with better intonation (see page 53).

Great bargains

When buying an acoustic guitar you may come across great bargains: Guitars sometimes sound and play as if they're worth at least twice or three times their actual price. It may take someone with experience to recognize an instrument like that. So when you go out to buy your first instrument, take a guitarist along — a good one, preferably, who can also tell the poorer-quality guitars that cost just as much, or more.

Why an expensive one?

Spotting the difference between low-budget and expensive guitars isn't that easy, especially since the quality of lower-priced instruments has improved a lot over the years. What exactly are you paying for when you spend more money on a guitar? Basically, you spend your money on better materials, better workmanship, and thus a better sound.

Finish and more

Also, more expensive guitars often have higher-quality finish and parts, such as the tuning machines. Or the rosette may have an intricate, finely-detailed inlay, and the markers of a steel-string guitar may be beautifully worked-out designs, instead of your basic dots — things that do little or nothing for the sound but add a lot to the instrument's exclusivity, or its beauty, and to its price, of course.

34

Handmade

Even two or three hundred dollar guitars are often advertised as 'handmade'. Are they, really? That depends on what you take handmade to mean. Many low-budget Spanish guitars, for example, are indeed built by hand, but in a mass production facility. When guitarists talk about 'real' handmade guitars, they refer to master *luthiers* who build a guitar from scratch, selecting and combining all the individual parts for sound and color. To complete the picture, there are also high-quality guitar companies that emphasize their extensive use of machines, explaining that they permit greater precision and consistency than human hands.

The intricately inlaid rosette of a classical guitar.

Concert guitars, student guitars?

The terms 'concert guitar' and 'student guitar' are just as confusing. After all, master luthiers build high-quality student guitars that cost a lot more than the so-called concert guitars made by anonymous guitar companies.

A good time

In the end you should buy the guitar that sounds and plays best for the price you're willing and able to pay. Some good news? In the lower and middle price ranges especially, quality has gone up and prices haven't. Whether a guitar is described as a handmade guitar, a concert guitar or student instrument is less important. What the audience mainly hears are the notes you play, and hardly anybody can or will tell the difference between a truly expensive instrument and something more affordable. What people *do* see

35

is that you're having a good time on stage, and buying the right guitar will definitely help you with that.

THE STORE

A music store with dozens of guitars to choose from can be quite intimidating, and it may be easier to select your guitar from a smaller collection. On the other hand, as testing guitars is largely a matter of comparing them, a wide selection is exactly what you need. It's equally important to find salespeople who enjoy their work and know what they're talking about. One more tip: Visit several music stores, and talk to a variety of salespeople, as they all have their own 'sound' too.

Time
Finally, take your time when buying an instrument — you'll probably have to live with it for years. On the other hand, you might end up buying the one guitar that you liked straightaway, after just the first few notes.

Buying online
You can also buy musical instruments online or by mail-order. This makes it impossible to compare instruments, of course, but most online and mail-order companies offer a return service for most or all of their products: If you're not happy with it, you can return it within a certain period of time. The instrument should be in new condition when you send it back.

PRE-OWNED GUITARS

A pre-owned guitar usually costs about half to two-thirds of its original price. For that kind of money it should be in good playing condition. Used guitars by well-known brands sell for more than

36

equally good guitars from unknown makes. You may want to take that into account when you buy a new one too.

Privately or in a store?

Purchasing a used instrument from a private individual may be cheaper than buying the same instrument from a store. One of the advantages of buying a used instrument in a store, though, is that you can go back if you have questions. Also, music stores may offer you a limited warranty on your purchase. Another difference is that a good dealer won't usually ask an outrageous price, but a private seller might — because he doesn't know any better, or because he thinks that you don't.

FOR MORE INFORMATION

If you want to know more, stock up on guitar magazines — which have reviews of the latest gear — and on all the brochures and catalogs you can find. Besides containing a wealth of information, the latter are designed to make you want to spend more than you have, or have in mind — so ask for a price list too. The Internet is another good source for up-to-date product information. And of course there are loads of other guitar books as well. You can find more about these resources beginning on page 179.

Fairs and conventions

One last tip: If a music trade show or convention is being held in your area, check it out. Besides a lot of instruments to try out and compare, you will also come across plenty of product specialists, as well as numerous fellow guitar players who are always a good source of information and inspiration.

5

A Good Guitar

Once you know what to look and listen out for, the differences between one guitar and another aren't that hard to spot. This chapter covers the technical aspects of the instrument, from types of wood to sizes, the fingerboard, the neck, and even the frets. The sound is dealt with also. Armed with this information, you're all set to buy the best guitar you can get.

The sound of a guitar depends to a large extent on the wood that has been used, and on the way it's been made. Chapters 7 and 8 are dedicated to the strings, which also play a major role.

Who's playing it

What a guitar sounds like also depends on who's playing it. If you haven't been playing that long, you won't be able to get the most out of an instrument. So if you really want to know what a guitar can sound like, have a good player play it — and that could very well be the salesperson.

Look or listen

This chapter starts with a closer look at the instrument. If you want to choose one by using your ears only, then skip ahead to page 66.

TIP

> ## Zippers and buckles
>
> *One more tip before you start testing guitars: Always be careful not to scratch the varnish with buckles, zippers, buttons, and bracelets.*

Finishes

Most classical guitars look pretty much alike, whereas steel-string guitars offer more variety in terms of appearance. Besides

... a wide variety of bridge designs.

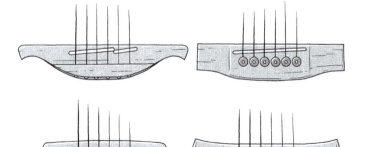

variations in the size and color of the bodies, you'll also find different types of varnish (high-gloss, silky gloss or matte, for instance) and a wide range of pickguard, head, and bridge designs.

Varnish
Color is a matter of taste; the quality of the varnish isn't. See if it has been applied evenly, and if there aren't any bubbles, stripes or drips. Look at the reflection too. If the guitar has a (silky) gloss varnish, the shine will tell you how well the various coats have been polished. Most guitars, including low-budget instruments, will pass these tests flawlessly. Do note that thick coats of varnish slow down the vibrations of the soundboard, restricting the instrument's sound.

Types of varnish
Until the 1970s, guitars were often finished with cellulose varnish, made of natural materials that allow the wood to breathe. This type of varnish also allows for invisible repairs. Today, cellulose varnish is used only on some expensive guitars. The majority of instruments are finished with a hard, synthetic-based varnish (e.g., polyurethane); alcohol-based and water-based varnishes are also used.

Pickguards
Pickguards protect the finish of your instrument. They come in lots of different colors and designs. Most of them are plastic. Unlike the traditional pickguard material (i.e., celluloid) they don't warp or expand. If you don't like the looks of a pickguard, get an instrument with a transparent one. Do note that a heavy pickguard restricts the vibrations of the top — and thus the sound — of your instrument.

Inlay
Classical guitars often have more intricately worked rosettes than steel-string instruments. Some cheap instruments have the rosette glued on, rather than inlaid.

Markers
The inlaid position markers on the fingerboards of steel-string

guitars vary from simple dots to elaborate abalone (mother-of-pearl) inlays.

> ### Markers on classical guitars
>
> *If you see a classical guitar with position markers (never on the fretboard, but on the side of the neck), it probably wasn't built in Spain. Markers on non-Spanish classical guitars usually mark the fifth, seventh and ninth (or sometimes tenth) positions. The soundbox starts at the twelfth fret.*

THE BODY

A guitar's sound is, to a significant degree, determined by the body. By its size, for one thing, at least when it comes to steel-string guitars; classical guitars are pretty much all the same size.

Classical guitars
The dimensions of different classical guitars vary hardly at all. That goes both for the size of the body and for the so-called *speaking length* of the strings, measured from the nut to the saddle. This *scale* (see pages 58–60) is usually a little over 25.5".

For children...
Smaller designs do exist, however. For younger children there are ¾ and ½-size guitars, with scales of around 24" (61 cm) and 23" (58 cm), respectively. Even smaller models are available too. As you can tell from their dimensions, ½ guitars are not half as big as regular instruments. Note that these *fractional* instruments are often tuned a bit higher. With standard tuning, string tension would be too low. Various companies make special strings for small guitars, compensating for this difference.

... and for ladies
Female players may consider a so-called señorita guitar, an

instrument with a slightly diminished scale and a narrower neck. Other small nylon-string instruments are used mainly for specific styles of music. Please refer to Chapter 13 for more information.

Ergonomic design

Guitars aren't the most comfortable instruments to play, which inspired at least one guitar maker to produce a complete line of ergonomically designed models.

TIP

Steel-string guitars

Steel-string guitars come with soundboxes in various sizes and shapes. The basic rule is very simple: A bigger body gives you a bigger sound. In other words, you'll get more volume, a broader, richer, deeper tone, and more low-end. That said, you may come across large guitars that sound disappointingly thin and small, and small guitars that sound remarkably big.

Too deep

The sound of a guitar can be too deep or too big as well, making it slow and sluggish. Likewise, a strong bass sound may be great when playing acoustically, but those low frequencies can get in your way when playing amplified or in a recording session. Many players perform smaller guitars in studio situations: There's no need for extra decibels, and it's often easier to control the sound of a smaller instrument.

Tipcode AGTR-004
Most guitarists prefer a larger size guitar for strumming.

TIPCODE

43

Dreadnought and Jumbo

Two well-known, large steel-string models are the Dreadnought, with an almost rectangular body shape, and the Jumbo. A Jumbo is much wider than a Dreadnought at the lower bout, but much narrower at the waist. The resulting rounded shape is reflected in the sound of the instrument, which is often described as being a bit 'rounder' than that of the average Dreadnought. The latter is the most popular steel-string model, especially among strumming guitar players around the world.

The right size

Considering the size of the soundbox of a new guitar is not about sound only. You should also take your down dimensions into consideration. When you're relatively small, a big guitar can easily be too big, making playing uncomfortable.

Jumbo

Dreadnought

Grand Auditorium (0000)

Auditorium (000)

Grand Concert (00)

Concert (0)

44

Grand Auditorium and Auditorium

The Grand Auditorium, also known as small Jumbo, is one of the most versatile steelstring guitars. The Auditorium is of course a little smaller again.

Singer-songwriters

Grand Auditorium and Auditorium models are often used by Singer-songwriters, folk guitarists and fingerpickers. They have a faster response than the larger guitars; their sound typically has stronger mids and better definition.

TIP

Fingerpicking

Fingerpickers play a bass line with their thumb while the other fingers play the melody. You literally 'pick' the strings, in a way similar to the classical guitar technique. Classical guitarists, however, use a technique that's commonly known as fingerstyle. Fingerpicking is used in various styles, ranging from bluegrass to folk. Some players use fingerpicks (see page 132), others play with their bare fingers. Flatpicking is another technique, using a flat pick to pick or strum the strings. Hybrid picking is a combination of both a flat pick and fingers.

Grand Concert and Concert

The soundbox of a Grand Concert guitar (00) is about as big as that of a classical guitar, and Concert guitars (0) are slightly

Tipcode AGTR-005
Fingerpicking guitarists play both a bass line and the melody.

TIPCODE

45

smaller. These easily playable models typically have a very light and open sound.

Zeros
The four guitar 'sizes' mentioned above are also indicated by one or more zeros. From large to small, the Grand Auditorium is a 0000, the Auditorium is a 000 ('Triple O'), and Grand Concert and Concert sizes equal 00 and 0 models, respectively.

Parlor
Concert and Grand Concerts are sometimes referred to as parlor guitars, though these instruments may have an even narrower upper bout. The name, parlor, indicates that such guitars are designed to be played for small audiences only.

Orchestra Model
The Orchestra Model or Orchestral Model (OM) is basically a Grand Auditorium with a wider neck and a longer scale (see pages 58–60). To make longer strings sound at the required pitch, they need more tension — and that's what promotes the bigger, powerful sound of this type of guitar.

Per brand
The exact dimensions of a certain type of guitar is different from guitar maker to guitar maker. The Grand Concert of one company can be more like a 000 than a 00; there are Dreadnoughts with wider and narrower waists, and so on. New models are introduced from time to time. The Grand Symphony, sometimes described as a cross between a Triple-O and a Jumbo, is just one example.

Acronyms
Many guitar makers use acronyms (D, J, GA, GC, OM) in their model names, referring to the original guitar models (D for Dreadnought, J for Jumbo, etc.).

Fiberglass body
Ovation was the first brand to introduce a guitar with a round, fiberglass back, appropriately named the *roundback*. There are roundbacks with nylon and steel-strings, with deep and shallow

bodies, and also with bodies made of other materials. Roundbacks have a very specific sound, and they're almost always acoustic-electric instruments.

Roundback.

Cutaway

A cutaway makes it easier to play the highest frets. Some brands offer certain models with or without a cutaway. Whether or not the difference can be heard has been debated for years. Some say the treble section sounds a bit brighter, due to the fact that the soundboard is smaller and therefore stiffer in that area; others feel that this fact actually reduces the trebles — and those are just two examples of the differences of opinion that exist, so listen and decide for yourself. A *Tip*: The difference between two identical non-cutaway guitars can easily be bigger than the difference between two identical guitars, one with a cutaway and one without.

TIP

The opposite

Most acoustic-electric guitars have a cutaway, and the inverse is also true: Guitars with a cutaway are usually acoustic-electric instruments.

Florentine and Venetian

Cutaways are most common on steel-string guitars, but you may also find them on nylon-string models. They come in different shapes. The ones that end in a sharp point are known as Florentine cutaways, as opposed to the Venetian version, which has a rounded shape.

47

Florentine cutaway.

Venetian cutaway.

Guitar strap

If you play standing up as well, don't just try the guitar out sitting down. Strangely, most steel-string guitars have only one button to attach the strap to, at the tail. The other end of the strap is then attached to the head, using the lace that comes with the strap. Knot the lace around the head under the strings, just below the tuning machines of the E-strings. Never attach the strap to the tuning machine itself, as you can easily bend it. A tip: A second *strap button* can be screwed into the heel. Another tip: Have a specialized technician do that for you. A third tip: Classical guitars are not supposed to have strap buttons.

TOP, BACK, AND INSIDE

48

The strings make the top vibrate, and those vibrations largely determine the sound of a guitar. This is what makes the top or *face* one of the most important parts of the instrument — and it also explains why it's known as the soundboard.

Solid

Guitars have either a *solid* or a *laminated top.* A solid top usually consists of a single piece of wood that has been split into two parts, much like a book that has been opened — hence the name *bookmatched* top.

Laminated

A laminated top, usually found on cheaper guitars, is made of plywood — a number of thin plies of wood that are glued together.

Better response

A solid-top guitar responds better to how loudly or how softly you play, or to how you strike the string (nails, fingertips, or a pick) and where (at the bridge or at the neck), for example. Guitars with laminated tops often seem to have a bit less life to them, producing a shallower and less dynamic sound. Solid-top guitars usually start around two to three hundred dollars, but you may find them for even less money.

Sound

Contrary to what you might think, a solid-top instrument won't always sound better than one with a laminated top. There are instruments around which have laminated tops but still sound good, and there are guitars with solid tops that you're better off not buying.

Traveling

A guitar with a laminated top may not sound as musical as one with a solid tip, but laminated wood can handle changes in temperature and relative humidity much better. So if you want to take a guitar on a camping trip, for example, it might be wise to choose a (low-budget) laminated top instrument.

49

The edge of the soundhole

A solid top can be recognized by looking at the edge of the soundhole. If the wood grain of the top continues beyond the edge, then you're looking at solid wood.

Fine, even grains

The quality of the wood itself is important too, as well as the way it has been sawed, the overall thickness of the top, the structure, and so on. Top-of-the-range instruments often have thin soundboards, with a fine, even grain and a uniform hue — but there are top-of-the-range instruments that look nothing like that at all.

Slightly convex

While you're looking at the top, also look at it sideways. A good top is often slightly convex, though this will hardly be visible. A guitar with an obviously convex top is probably better left well alone, and the same goes for an instrument with a sagging, concave top.

TIP

Quarter-sawn wood

Good instruments usually have a top made of quarter-sawn wood (see page 175). This method of sawing wood makes for thin, yet strong tops that are less sensitive to changes in the humidity level, reducing the risk of cracking. Slab-cutting wood is more cost-effective. It takes a trained eye to distinguish the two.

Cedar or spruce

Most guitar tops are made of either cedar or spruce. Both are conifers, yet they have different characteristics. They also look different. Cedar is usually brown, while spruce is much lighter, almost white in color. (Other types of wood are also used, such as cypress for flamenco guitars.)

How they sound

Most guitarists find the sound of a guitar with a cedar top a bit

50

warmer, deeper, and rounder, while spruce tops are often said to sound a little brighter. Don't be surprised, however, if you hear an expert stating the opposite. Spruce is more commonly used for steel-string guitars and flamenco guitars. The American or Canadian Sitka spruce is especially popular among steel-string guitar luthiers. Cedar is more often used for classical guitars, though other woods such as the European Alpine spruce may also be used.

Back and sides

When it comes to the sound of the instrument, the back and sides are less important than the top. To prove that, the well-known luthier Torres (see page 146) once made a guitar with a back and sides of papier-mâché. He told no one, played it, and everybody loved it…
On the other hand, there are guitarists who say they can even hear the difference between a two- and a three-part back.

Laminated or solid

Most guitars have laminated backs and sides, but instruments with a body made entirely of solid wood are also available, for prices under and well over a thousand dollars.

Wood type

Mahogany is often used for the backs and sides of less expensive guitars. A colored varnish may be used to make it look like the more expensive (Rio) rosewood you find on better guitars. Rosewood is said to promote full rich basses and transparent highs. Other types of wood commonly used include maple, for a tight, bright sound, and — in the higher price ranges — walnut or koa.

TIP

Different materials

Some makers employ entirely different materials for their instruments, such as bamboo rather than wood, and there are guitars made entirely of graphite, or instruments with a one-piece, plastic bracing system.

51

Size and material

The type of wood used may also depend on the size of the guitar. Some makers use maple for their larger models, for instance, because this hard type of wood adds some brightness to these bassier-sounding instrument. The harder the wood, the brighter the tone will be. Softer woods make for a mellower sound.

The inside too

Check the body, both inside and out, to see how well it has been finished. If you find gaps or big lumps of glue or varnish, it might give you cause to wonder if enough attention has been paid to the rest of the guitar. Also check that the neck and fingerboard connect seamlessly to the body, and that no craftsman's hand slipped while working with a file or a chisel. A high level of workmanship doesn't in itself guarantee a great-sounding guitar. Conversely, there are guitars that don't look good but sound wonderful. More often, though, the workmanship does tell you something about the all-around quality of the instrument you're looking at.

Bracing

Everything that's attached to the top determines how it vibrates. That, in turn, largely determines the sound of the guitar. A luthier can control the timbre of an instrument by varying the bracing pattern, for example, but also by using thinner, wider, higher, flatter, or scalloped braces. Each luthier has his own bracing 'recipe'.

Multiple soundholes (Ovation).

Soundhole

Likewise, the sound of a guitar can be influenced by the graduation of the top, or by the size and position of the soundhole. Some guitars even have unusually shaped soundholes, or more than one.

GOOD NECK, GOOD FINGERBOARD

The neck and fingerboard are important to how a guitar plays and feels. To some extent, they help determine the sound as well.

Harder is brighter

The fingerboard is made of a hard type of wood. On less expensive guitars it's usually rosewood, with a dark-brown look Ebony, an almost black type of wood, is a popular choice for expensive guitars, being harder. The harder the wood of the fingerboard, the brighter and more direct the tone can be, and the fingerboard may have a smoother feel to it. Being so much harder, ebony fingerboards also last longer than rosewood boards. Rosewood fingerboards promote a warmer, milder, or drier tone.

The neck

Acoustic guitar necks are often made of mahogany, cedar, or (for lower budget instruments) nato, reinforced by a strip of the same or another type of wood, such as ebony.

Straight neck

The neck must be perfectly straight; it may not curve to the left or right. Check the neck by looking downwards from the head toward the body along the side of the fingerboard. You can check that the neck isn't twisted at the same time.

Intonation

At the twelfth fret, the strings should sound exactly one octave higher than when they are open — i.e., when you don't fret them. If they do not, your guitar has bad intonation.

53

Harmonics

Here's how you check this. Place a finger very lightly on the thick E-string, exactly above the twelfth fret, barely touching it, and then strike the string pretty hard, close to the bridge. What you'll hear — possibly only after some practice — is a high, thinnish tone, known as a *harmonic, overtone* or *flageolet*. Now press the same string to the twelfth fret, as you would in normal playing; you should get exactly the same pitch. Check the other strings in the same way.

TIPCODE

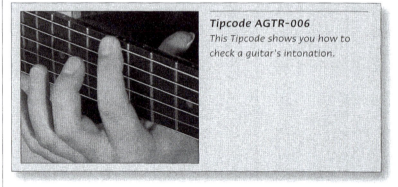

Tipcode AGTR-006
This Tipcode shows you how to check a guitar's intonation.

Not easy

At first, it may not be that easy to hear whether a harmonic sounds too high, too low or just right. A good electronic tuner (see pages 122–124) can help, but an experienced guitarist may be even more effective.

A different pitch

If the intonation is off, you'll have problems when playing with other musicians; your high notes will have a slightly different pitch than theirs. The higher the fret you're playing, the more out of tune you will be. Another problem? On a guitar like this your ears slowly get

TIP

Decent strings

Some cheap guitars are sold with strings that simply don't allow for proper intonation — even on a perfect guitar. A set of decent strings solves the problem, improving your sound as well for less than ten dollars.

used to the wrong pitches. You may not be too troubled by it until you switch to a good guitar, which can then sound out of tune, to you...

Dead spots

Another test is checking the instrument for *dead spots*. Play all the strings at all of the frets and listen for positions where a string sounds noticeably shorter, drier or softer.

Rattles

While you're at it, also check for rattles and buzzing sounds — especially on used guitars. Some unwanted noises may be noticeable only at certain pitches. Harmonics, which you can also play at a number of other frets (the fifth and the seventh, for example), can sometimes make otherwise inaudible sounds stand out. Another test? Gently tap the body with a fingertip or a knuckle and listen, or carefully shake the guitar. If you want to know more about rattles and buzzes, and their possible causes, check out pages 69–70.

Concave neck

A guitar neck should be slightly concave from the head to the body. To check this, press the low E-string simultaneously at both the first and the fifteenth fret. The middle of the string should now be floating just a little above the frets in the middle of the neck. If not, you've got a flat neck, or even a convex one, which may result in strings rattling against the frets. If there's more than about 1⁄32 (1 mm) between the string and the frets, the neck is too concave, making the guitar harder to play.

A third hand

If you're unable to see whether the string touches the frets, you'll need a third hand to strike it, so ask someone else to play the string while you fret it, or use a capo at the first fret (see pages 125–126). If the string is able to sound freely, everything's okay.

Adjustable necks

The necks of most steel-string guitars can be adjusted with the built-in truss rod (preferably leave this to a professional). Classical guitars are not adjustable in this way.

Bolt-on necks

Some acoustic guitars have bolt-on necks, rather than a traditional glued neck. Some of the main advantages of a bolt-on neck are the improved stability and serviceability.

MORE ABOUT NECKS

Steel-string guitars come with a wide variety of necks. There's also plenty to tell about the necks of classical guitars.

Wide

Classical guitars have pretty wide fingerboards, measuring a little over two inches (5 cm) at the nut. The strings of these guitars are quite widely spaced, to allow for the techniques used in classical guitar music. When you're just starting out, a slightly narrower, thinner neck will be easier to play, but there aren't too many options to choose from.

Your thumb

Proper classical guitar technique requires you to rest the thumb of your left hand somewhere in the middle of the back of the neck. This makes it easier to stop the strings with the tips of your fingers, and it allows you to spread your fingers as widely as possible. The neck of the classical guitar has been designed for this purpose.

TIPCODE

Tipcode AGTR-007
This Tipcode demonstrates classical guitar technique, using the tips of the fingers to stop the strings.

Profile

The necks of many steel-string guitars, on the other hand, are designed to make playing chords easier. Most players have their thumbs higher on the back of the neck, just like electric-guitar players usually do.

Classical
left-hand
technique.

TIP

Easy transition

There are steel-string guitars with a very narrow neck and a low action, making for an easy transition from playing electric to playing acoustic. Likewise, there are nylon-string instruments with a slim neck and a cutaway, designed for steelstring players who like the sound, but not the feel of a classical nylon-string guitar.

D, C and V

The profile of a neck is hard to put into words. Using letters is easier; a neck with a D-profile has a rather flat back, while the letter C indicates a rounder profile. Necks with a 'sharper' V-profile are mainly used by guitarists who fret the sixth string, or even the fifth string, with their left thumb. This slightly pointed profile allows your thumb to fit more easily around it. Fingerpickers tend to like this type of neck too. Most of them also prefer the slightly wider string spacing that comes with a broader neck.

Radius

Steel-string guitars, like most electric guitars, have fingerboards

57

that are a bit higher underneath the middle strings and gently slope down toward the thin and thick strings. This rounding, called *radius* or *camber*, makes it easier to finger chords.

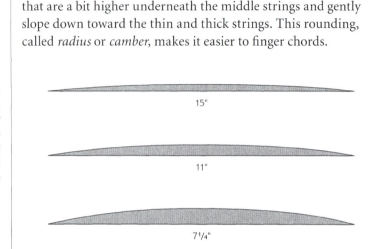

15"

11"

7¹⁄₄"

Flat or round?

The radius is expressed in inches. The higher the number, the flatter the fingerboard. Most steel-string guitars have a radius of twelve inches. A fingerboard with a *compound radius* is a bit rounder at the nut than at the last fret.

Neck widths

There's more variation in the width of the neck among steel-string guitars than among classical guitars. The necks are usually between 1 ¹³⁄₁₆" and 1 ¹³⁄₁₆" wide at the nut (42-46 mm), getting wider toward the neck and usually ending up slightly over 2" (5 cm). If you play mainly chords, a narrower fingerboard makes things easier. For other playing techniques, such as fingerpicking, many guitarists prefer a wider neck.

THE SCALE

When an open string is struck, it vibrates between the nut and the saddle. This vibrating part is called the speaking length of the string. This equals the *scale* of the guitar, which is used to indicate its size. On steel-string guitars the scale usually varies from a little under 25" to about 26" (62.5–66 cm). Most classical guitars have a scale of a little over 25.5" (65 cm).

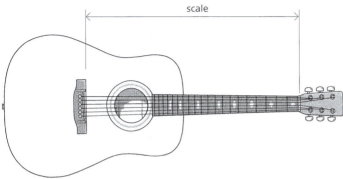

scale

The scale is the length of the strings measured from the saddle to the nut.

Tighter
The longer the scale, the further apart the frets will be, so the more you have to spread your fingers. Also, the strings have to be wound a little tighter to sound the same pitch. This increased tension helps produce a broader, fuller sound and a little more volume. Fingerpicking guitarists often choose long-scale guitars.

Acoustic bass guitars
Most acoustic guitars have four strings, each tuned one octave below the equivalent (lowest-sounding) four strings of a 'regular' guitar. Short strings can't go that low and still sound good, so

Acoustic bass guitars have longer scales.

59

that's why bass guitars have much longer scales, up to around 34"
(86 cm).

Decide for yourself

Guitarists with big hands often — but not always — prefer a thick
neck to a slim one, and vice versa. Some guitarists would rather
play on a flat, thick neck with a round fingerboard. Other guitarists
prefer a round, slim neck with a flatter fingerboard. Sometimes
these choices are based on the music they play, and sometimes
they're not. The message: Watch and listen to what other guitarists
are doing, but decide for yourself what suits you best.

Fourteen-fret and twelve-fret necks

Most steel-string guitars have a fourteen-fret neck, meaning that
the body starts at the fourteenth fret. These necks seem to be
longer than twelve-fret necks, but that's not the difference. In fact,
the difference lies in the soundbox: Guitars with a twelve-fret neck
have a longer soundbox, 'reaching out' to the twelfth fret, as it
were. This can make for a slightly bigger, rounder sound, with the
drawback that it's harder to play the highest positions. Another
difference: The necks of twelve-fret models are often a bit wider.

A choice of necks

You've found a great guitar, but you're not happy about the neck?
Usually, that would be a problem, but some expensive series come
with a choice of necks, as well as a choice of different position
markers and other inlays.

ACTION

The action of a guitar refers to the distance between the strings
and the fingerboard. A guitar with a high action has its strings
rather high above the fingerboard, and vice versa.

Too high, too low

The higher the action, the heavier the guitar will play; you have to press the strings down quite far before they touch the frets. If the action is too low, the strings will rattle against the frets (*string buzz* or *fret buzz*). Flamenco guitarists often produce that rattling sound intentionally, by playing with a very low action and fiercely attacking the strings with their nails.

From high to low

On new guitars the action is more often on the high than on the low side. That makes sense, as it's easier to lower a high action than it is to raise a low one. An action that's too high can also be remedied temporarily — when you're trying out guitars, for instance.

A capo

A guitar with a very high action is hard to judge. The temporary solution? A *capo*, which is a clamp that you can mount anywhere on the neck. Capos are really designed to raise the pitch of the guitar in half steps (see page 126), but they can also be used to temporarily lower the action. For that purpose, you capo the first fret. This will make the guitar sound a half step higher, but what really counts at this stage is that it's comfortable to play.

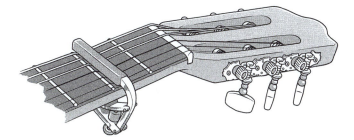

A capo, shown here in the second position. Like most other models, this capo can also be mounted the other way around.

Adjusting the action

Of course you can't leave the capo on the guitar forever, and you won't need to either. A technician can adjust the action by lowering the nut or the saddle, or, conversely, by replacing them

61

with taller models. On steel-string guitars, the truss rod may have to be adjusted as well.

Nylon-string action

A classical guitar is considered to have a low action if the distance between the twelfth fret and the thick E-string is about 9⁄64" (3.5 mm) or less. If there's more than about 3⁄16" (4.75 mm) clearance, the action is considered high — but there are great classical guitars with an action of more than 4⁄16" (6.35 mm). The action on the low E-string is usually a bit higher than on the high E-string; thick strings need more space to move. If the overall action is too low, the sound may suffer.

Steel-string action

Steel-string guitars have a lower overall action. Usually there's about 1⁄16" under the high E (1.5 mm) and a bit more under the low E (5⁄64" or 2 mm). If you use a slide rather than stopping the strings with your fingers (see page 125), you'll probably want a higher action.

TUNING MACHINES

Tuning machines — also known as *machine heads*, *tuning heads* or *tuning gears* — should wind easily and smoothly, have no play, and produce no buzzes or rattles. On classical guitars they're

Sealed tuners on a steel-string guitar.

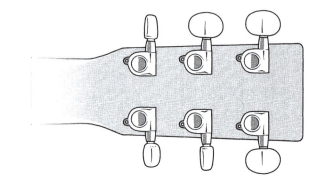

always open, while most steel-string guitars have enclosed tuners, encased by a metal housing. These sealed tuners are usually self-lubricating; there's no need to oil them.

Gear ratios

Tuning machines can also differ in what 'gear' they're in. If you have 10:1 tuners, the posts that wind the string turn around once for every ten times you turn the key.

Tuning is easier and more precise with 14:1 or even 16:1 tuners. And if you've found a great guitar, but you're not happy about the tuning machines, they can be easily replaced.

The nut

Most modern guitars — even low-budget models —have decent tuning machines. Tuning problems? Have a look at the top nut first. The strings should be able to move freely through its notches (see page 65).

TIP

Gold-plated

Many steel-string guitars have gold-colored tuning machines instead of chrome-plated ones. That gold color may actually be brass, but there are also gold-plated tuning machines, and they're not as expensive as you might think. Thin gold plating can wear off quickly, though.

FRETS

Smooth and well-finished frets make for an easy-playing guitar that feels good in your hands. You may come across frets that are a little too short, resulting in E-strings that slip off of the fingerboard. If they're too long they jut out from the neck, which may indicate that the guitar has been stored in too dry an environment (see pages 138–140).

63

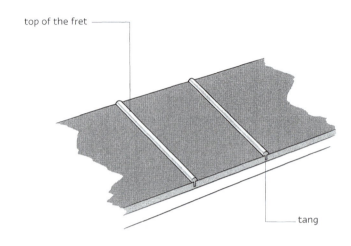

top of the fret

tang

Edgier frets, edgier sound

And yes, even frets influence the sound of an instrument. Frets with an edgier top make for an 'edgier' sound, while rounder frets can make the sound — you've got it — a little rounder.
If the frets are too high, it will be harder to slide from one position to the next. If they're too low, the strings will loose some of their tone.

Fretless basses

There are acoustic bass guitars that have a fretless neck, just like a double bass. Their timbre is described as having a 'singing' quality, and there's less attack in the sound. In order to play in tune, you have to stop the strings in exactly the right place, rather than anywhere between two frets. This is what makes playing fretless instruments quite a bit harder than fretted ones. Fretless guitars are very rare, but they do exist.

Two octaves

Nylon-string guitars usually have eighteen or nineteen frets. In addition, they sometimes have one or two half frets beside the soundhole, for the very highest notes. Steel-string guitars usually have twenty frets. On some guitars you'll find a twenty-fourth fret, for the high E and B-strings. This allows you to play two octaves on those strings — but it isn't easy.

64

BRIDGE SADDLE AND NUT

Most bridge saddles and nuts are made of a hard synthetic material designed to pass on the vibrations of the strings to the guitar as well as possible. They used to be made of ivory. Many players love bone nuts and saddles, which can be found on more expensive guitars.

Compensated saddles

Steel-string guitars often have a *compensated saddle*; the saddle is not at a 90° angle to the strings, as it is on most classical guitars. Compensated saddles are designed to improve a guitar's intonation, making it sound in tune in each and every position. Some saddles even consist of two or more parts, for the same reason.

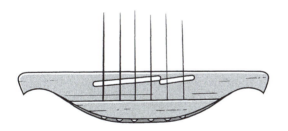

A compensated saddle.

How it works

If you stop a string, you shorten its speaking length. Pressing it down also increases string tension. This makes the pitch go up more than required. The compensated saddle solves the problem. Nylon-string guitars don't have a compensated saddle: Nylon strings respond differently to the extra tension.

The nut

If you're playing an instrument and the strings keep getting stuck while you're tuning, the slots or notches in the nut might be too narrow. A temporary solution? Repeatedly press the string you're tuning just behind the nut. If this happens with your own guitar, please refer to pages 126–127 for additional tips.

65

WHAT TO LISTEN FOR

Besides dead spots and poor intonation, there's a lot more to listen for. Here are some more tips for judging guitars with your ears.

A wall works well

When you're playing, you don't hear the same sound as your audience does. You can come close, though. Just sit down facing a wall so that the sound of the guitar bounces back to you. Another solution? Ask the salesperson to play a few different guitars, or take somebody with you who can play them for you. A little distance may help you to judge the sound and the character of the instrument better.

Balanced

A good guitar is well-balanced in terms of volume, tone, and sustain. The low strings shouldn't be louder than the high ones, nor the other way around. Because they're wound, the low strings not only sound lower than the high ones, they also sound different. They shouldn't sound too different, however.

The third string

On nylon-string guitars, the sound of the third string (G) often deviates. Being the heaviest plain string, it sounds much less bright than the D, which is the thinnest wound string. Some strings and string sets have been designed to reduce this effect (see pages 85–86).

Sustain

The thin strings don't sustain as long as the thick ones, and in higher positions the sustain will get shorter — but it should be balanced, and never get too short. Play some chords, let them ring, and listen to what happens. Some guitars sustain much longer than others. If you play fast licks or funky chords only, sustain is less important.

Dynamics

Something else to listen to is a guitar's range from loud to soft: the dynamics. The guitar should have a beautiful, full tone even at its quietest, and it should sound just as good when you play it really loud. The best check? Play it the way you're going to play it — but do remember that it's not yours yet.

Taste

Other than that, it's mostly a matter of taste and the style of music you play. You can go for a bright sound, or you may prefer something warmer. The heavy basses that one player loves may sound too boomy to another. Some guitars have a very transparent sound; when you play a chord, you can hear every single string separately. Other instruments have a thicker, heavier, solid type of sound.

Transparent

A guitar with a transparent sound will often sound quite bright, with lots of highs. A nasal-sounding guitar may sound blocked in one way, but it may offer the perfect timbre for some situations...

Deep or shallow

One guitar might have a deep, rich sound, while another may have a shallow, less articulate or dynamic tone. A shallow sound may not be unpleasant at first, but it can become boring after a while.

Personal taste

When two people listen to the same guitar, they may use very different words to describe what they hear. What one finds harsh (in other words, unpleasant), another may describe as bright (in other words, pleasant), and what's warm to one ear sounds dull to another. It all depends on what you like, and on the words you use to describe sound.

TIP

Don't look

When selecting the guitars you want to listen to, you'll almost automatically look at the price as well. Chances are that you will hear that price too.
A solution? Let the salesperson hand you a number of guitars in your price range, one by one. Don't look. Just play them, one by one. And listen.

67

Three

When you're trying to choose the best of a whole bunch of guitars, it's easy to get confused. A tip? Pick out three guitars, based on the salesperson's advice or your own ears. Play them. Then swap the one you like least for another instrument. Listen. And so on.

Turn around

If you've found a couple of guitars that feel good and play well, and you intend to choose between them on the basis of their sound only, ask someone to play the same piece of music on each guitar. If you really want to go only for the sound, and not for looks, the brand name, or other elements that do more to your mind than to the instrument's tone, turn around so that you can't see which guitar is being played.

No two are alike

Just as no two trees are ever the same, you'll never find two guitars that sound exactly alike. Not even if they're of the same brand and the same series, and built the same day by the same person. So it's advisable to always play the guitar you're going to buy, and to buy the guitar which you played, instead of an 'identical' one from the stockroom.

Longer

A guitar often starts to sound its best after you've played it for fifteen or twenty minutes. Only then does the instrument really open up, as some would say. Another explanation is that it takes you about twenty minutes to get to know a guitar to the point where you can make it sound better.

TWELVE-STRING GUITARS

A twelve-string guitar has six double string courses. The lowest sounding four strings (E, A, D, G) have an extra string that sound an octave higher; the highest two strings (B, E) have an extra string that sounds the same pitch. The extra strings make for the instrument's characteristic ringing sound. Some tips.

- The **twelve strings** pull the neck really hard. As a result, the guitar's action can easily be too high. Check its playability and don't forget to play the high positions too.

- The strings of each course should not be too far apart. If the **spacing** is too wide, it will be hard to stop a course without touching or even stopping adjacent strings.

- Twelve-string guitars have a somewhat **wider neck**, but it's not a wide as a traditional nylon-string neck.

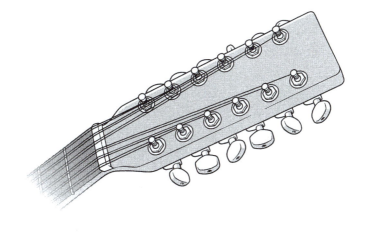

The head of a twelve-string guitar.

PRE-OWNED INSTRUMENTS

When you're considering a pre-owned guitar, there are a few things that need extra attention.

- Check the body, the neck, and the fingerboard for **cracks and other damage**.

- Damage is caused not only by bumps and falls, but also by dry air or by sudden changes in **air humidity** (see pages 138–140).

- **Small cracks in the varnish** may indicate that a guitar has been stored in a very dry environment, just like frets that jut out from the neck.

69

- Also pay attention to **seams and joints**, for example between fingerboard and body.

- Listen for things you don't want to hear. Some **rattles or buzzes** may be easily corrected, perhaps by fastening a strap button, replacing a string whose winding has come undone, or, on a classical guitar, cutting a piece of string that is buzzing against the top, right behind the bridge. If a string is broken, its tuning machine may buzz.

- There are other **sounds** that you won't be able to get rid of, unless you have the instrument repaired by a specialist. A loose brace, a pickguard that's come loose, an invisible crack in the body, a loose nut…

- **Worn-out frets** can make your strings buzz, and they impede string-bending. Frets can be replaced or refinished.

Worn-out frets impede string bending.

- Poor intonation may be the result of **an old set of strings**.

- The tiniest drop of oil can makes **open tuning machines** run smoothly again. Inferior or old ones can be replaced, if the guitar is worth it.

- A good used guitar can last **years and years** more.
- On acoustic-electric guitars, check to see if all the **controls** are working well, and make sure they don't creak. Creaking is often easily solved with contact spray, but even then you have to know what you're doing.

- A final tip, to underline an earlier point: **Take somebody along** who knows about guitars, especially if you're buying from a private seller.

70

Vintage instruments

Vintage violins can cost well over a million dollars. Guitars have yet to become that expensive, but there are vintage instruments that cost at least as much as new ones of similar quality. This has to do with older instruments being rare, and partly with the fact that the sound of a good guitar may well improve with age. If you're interested in vintage guitars, check out *Vintage Guitar magazine* (see page 181) and consult the vintage acoustic guitars buying guide that you can find online.

6

Acoustic-Electric Guitars

Only if it's really quiet, like at a classical guitar concert, will the sound of an acoustic guitar be loud enough to fill a concert hall. Quite often, you'll need a little or a lot more volume. That's where acoustic-electric guitars come in.

Most acoustic-electric guitars don't look any different from a regular steel-string guitar — and they're often the same instruments, apart from the built-in electronics. As said before, acoustic-electric usually have a cutaway, and instruments with a cutaway are usually acoustic-electrics.

Control panel
Other than that, you can recognize most acoustic-electrics by the small control panel for the preamplifier, located on the left upper bout, or in the soundhole.

Pickup
The pickup or *transducer* is usually a *piezo pickup* — a very thin, small strip which can be hidden under the bridge saddle.

An undersaddle piezo pickup.

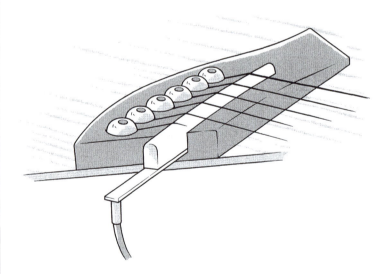

Input jack
The cable is plugged in the input jack, located in the strap button at the tail of the instrument.

Prices
Acoustic-electric guitars, with either steel or nylon strings, come in a wide variety of prices. The cheapest models start at as low as two or three hundred dollars. More money buys you a better

74

guitar, a better pickup/preamp combination, or both. Quite a few brands offer you a choice of pickup systems by different makers.

A microphone

Some systems feature both an undersaddle piezo pickup and a small microphone to round off the sound. The sound of a piezo pickup is usually said to be rather clean; the microphone, clipped on the edge of the soundhole or mounted inside, provides a more natural, warm sound. With such systems, the balance between the two can usually be adjusted: more piezo if feedback (see below) is a problem, more microphone if it's not, for instance.

Microphone under the bridge

As an alternative to piezo pickups, there are also flat 'microphones' that can be installed under the bridge saddle, similar to a piezo.

TIP

Shallow bodies

Another category of acoustic-electrics are the instruments that are built solely for amplified playing. They're usually nylon strung. The shallow body hardly, if at all, acts as a soundbox, and they may have some type of grill rather than a conventional soundhole.

Feedback problems

Acoustic-electric guitars are notorious for causing *feedback*; the loud *skreee* you also hear if you accidentally point a microphone at a loudspeaker. The deeper and larger the guitar's body and the louder you play, the more likely you are to have feedback problems.

Solutions

There are many ways to fight or prevent feedback.

• **A notch filter**, which may be found on the preamp control panel of your guitar or on your guitar amplifier, combats feedback by filtering the relevant frequency out of the sound.

75

- Contrary to a notch filter, a **phase switch** does not influence the sound. If your guitar and or your amp has a phase switch, always see what it does to fight feedback before using a notch filter.

- An acoustic way to stop feedback is simply to **reposition yourself**, your instrument, and/or your amp and speakers.

- You can also close **the soundhole** of your guitar with a rubber disc, known as a *feedback buster* or some such name. Wooden soundhole covers, some with intricate carvings, are available too.

Volume and tone

The control panel of an acoustic-electric usually features both volume and tone controls. (usually a two or three band EQ, featuring controls for bass and treble, or bass, treble, and mids). Some preamps offer more extensive tone controls, or allow you to adjust the brilliance of the sound.

A nylon-string acoustic-electric with a shallow body.

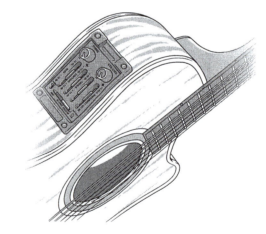

Effects and tuners

Various preamplifiers also offer effects. Most commonly a reverb, adding depth and space to the sound, but there are preamps with a built-in delay, chorus, and other effects. Some come with user presets to store various settings, or a built-in electronic tuner.

76

Soundhole preamp

Various companies make preamps that are installed into the soundhole, so there's no need for a hole in the guitar's bout. A soundhole preamp makes it a bit harder to reach your controls or check their positions, but many guitarist prefer the looks of a guitar without a control panel in the upper bout.

Invisible

You can also consider a preamp without on-board controls. Some systems have the preamp built in a small tube, attached to the input jack/strap button. One major advantage is that they don't require a hole to be made in the side of your instrument. The battery is mounted in a small clamp close to the soundhole. Unwinding the strings provides enough space to replace it.

External preamp

The preamp can also be built into the plug of your instrument cable, or you can use an external preamp. These are great solutions if you don't want any work done to your instrument. A disadvantage is that you can't control volume or tone from your guitar.

Battery check

Built-in preamps are powered by a battery. A check light on the control panel warns you when power runs low. You'll hear that as well, as the sound will get progressively worse.

How long?

It's hard to predict how long preamp batteries last, as it depends both on the type of battery you're using and on the preamp itself. Expect a minimum of some hundred playing hours, but your battery may also last a thousand hours or more. The electronics of

TIP

Unplug your instrument

Always unplug the instrument as soon as you stop playing. This switches the preamp off. If you don't, your batteries won't last long.

77

older acoustic-electrics typically use more energy, reducing battery life.

Retrofitting

Pickups and preamps can be retrofit as well — preferably by a specialized technician. A pickup that's not properly installed may cause feedback problems, for one thing. The prices of pickups and preamps vary a lot, as does the cost of having them built in. If you want really good results, count on spending about two to three hundred dollars or more, everything included. Some of the better known brands in this area are Ashworth, B-Band, EMG, EPM, Fishman, Highlander, Lace, L.R. Baggs, Shadow, Schaller, and Seymour Duncan.

Which guitar?

Basically you can turn any guitar into an acoustic-electric, but many guitarists prefer a model with a body that's not too big, in order to minimize feedback problems. The Grand Concert size is a popular choice.

Magnetic pickup

If your steel-string guitar needs to be amplified just once in while, you can go for a magnetic pickup that can be mounted in the soundhole, using clips or clamps, or adhesive tape. Prices range from some fifty dollars to four times as much, and more. Note that magnetic pickups don't respond to nylon strings. *Tip:* The quality of soundhole pickups has gone up considerably!

Microphone

Regular microphones are usually used in studios. Onstage you risk feedback, and you'll have to keep your guitar quite still, aiming the soundhole at the microphone. A clip-on microphone, as described above, buys you the freedom to move around. There are also ultra-flat microphones that can be stuck onto or inside the body, so that no holes have to be drilled.

Acoustic amplifiers

Unlike amplifiers for electric guitars, which contribute a lot to the sound of the instrument, amps for acoustic guitars are supposed to only amplify the sound — to make it louder, not to alter it. These special amps are known as *acoustic amplifiers*, contradictory as that may sound. Most well-known amplifier manufacturers offer one or more types.

Power ratings

The smallest acoustic amps have a power output of some 15 or 25 watts RMS, which is enough for only the very smallest venues. Such amps are available for less than a hundred dollars. Need more power? Expect to pay some five or six hundred dollars for a decent amp of 40 to 50 watts. Power output, sound quality, and features can only go up from there, with prices of more than three thousand dollars. If you play in a band with other amplified instruments, you'll soon be needing up to 100 watts or more, unless there's a PA system.

An acoustic amplifier (SWR).

79

Combo

Acoustic amplifiers are usually *combo amplifiers* or *combos*, with one or more small loudspeakers (often only 5" or 8") and an amplifier all in one box. Some models come with a bigger speaker combined with a dedicated tweeter that looks like a small horn, for the highest frequencies. Each combo has its own sound, so always listen to a couple of them before buying one, and preferably use your own guitar to play-test them.

Effects

Most amps have one or more built-in effects. A reverb is a welcome addition, especially if you use the same amp for vocals as well; many amps feature a microphone input, since many guitar players sing too. Another popular built-in effect is *chorus*, which doubles the sound and gives it a fuller, more dynamic and spacious feel. These and other effects are also available in dedicated effects units for acoustic instruments.*

PA

If you play larger venues, your guitar may be plugged directly into the PA mixer. If your amplifier has a DI (direct) output or a line output, you can plug your guitar into your amp and connect your amp to the mixer.*

Tips

- Always listen to acoustic-electrics **unamplified** (even those with a shallow body) **as well as amplified**.

- Audition acoustic-electric guitars with **your own amplifier**. If you don't have one (yet), be aware of the fact that no two amps sound the same.

- When you play the guitar amplified, does the sound only get louder or does the **tone** change as well?

- Acoustic-electric guitars often have a rather **low action and light strings**. Keep that in mind when you're trying them out.

- How sensitive is the guitar to **feedback**? It's easier to find that

* Want to know more? Read Tipbook Amplifiers and Effects (see page 232).

out when you compare a couple of guitars. Sit down with those guitars at different angles to the speakers — and don't open the amplifier up all the way.

• Check that the volume and tone controls work **evenly**, and across their entire range.

• Listen for **noise and hum**. If you hear any, the culprit may be the guitar, but it could also be the cable, the amp, or other electrical systems in the room.

• Check if **the battery** is easily replaceable.

7

Strings

If you want to get the most out of your instrument, you need to know a bit about strings. Strings are extremely important for how your guitar plays and sounds, and there's a wide variety of strings to choose from.

Strings sound best when you fit them properly, and they'll sound good longer if you keep them clean. Chapter 8 deals with both subjects.

Tension

Steel-strings put quite a lot of tension on your guitar — a force comparable to the weight of a fully-grown guitar player. Nylon-string guitars are designed to cope with about half that tension. If you put steel-strings on a nylon-string guitar, the top may crack, the bridge may come loose, or the neck may warp, to name just a few of the risks.

Nylon on steel

Putting nylon strings on a steel-string guitar is not a good idea either. The posts are not designed for nylon strings, and the strings lack the amount of tension that you'd need to make the sound-board vibrate sufficiently. The result? Not much at all, really.

Which strings

The only way to find out exactly which brand or series of strings you like best on your guitar is to try them out. A knowledgeable salesperson may help you narrow down the extensive choice some-what.
Describe the type of sound you're looking for and the music you're playing, and he or she will be able to suggest a few types and brands that may match your taste.

Websites

You can also check out the websites or brochures of guitar string makers. Some of them offer lots of helpful information on the sound characteristics of the various types of strings they make.

TIP

Your current strings

Tip: Jot down which strings you're currently using on page 227, so you can buy them again if you like them, or avoid them if you don't!

84

Cheap strings

It has been said before: Cheap guitars often come with cheap strings. Any decent set of strings will just as often improve the sound of the instrument, as well as its intonation (the latter especially with nylon strings).

NYLON STRINGS

Nylon strings are available in various tensions, windings, colors, types, and brands. Here are the basics.

Tensions

Most brands offer three choices when it comes to string tension, some four, and a few brands even more. Compared to normal- or low-tension strings, high tension strings feel a bit tighter and play a bit 'heavier', and the sound is a bit brighter and more articulate. Lower tension strings are easier to play, and they tend to produce a warmer, drier, less distinctive sound.

Wound strings

The three thickest strings consist of ultra-fine nylon wires that are twisted together (*floss nylon* or *multifilaments*) and wound with metal wire. The winding makes the strings heavier, which allows them to sound as low as they should.
If you were to use plain nylon wire (*monofilament*) for these strings, they'd have to be really thick, resulting in a dull, weak, tubby tone.

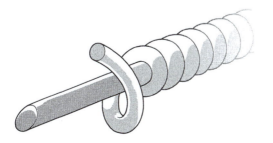

A wound string.

85

The third string

To an extent this is illustrated by the third string, the G. Being a bit on the heavy side for a plain nylon string, it tends to sound a bit muddy or tubby compared to its wound neighbor, the D. To reduce this difference, some brands offer wound third strings, or they use a different type of nylon. Some sets come with two G-strings: a regular one, and one made of a different material, so you can compare the two.

Silver, bronze, or gold-plated

Most wound strings have a silver-plated brass winding, which promotes a nice, bright tone. Bronze wound strings are often said to sound a bit warmer (if you like them) or less bright (if you don't). Strings with gold-plated brass windings sound good, but the brightness may not last that long, since gold is rather soft.

Clear, yellow, or black

Plain strings are usually made of clear transparent nylon, like fishing wire, but there are yellow and black ones too. Most experts say the color doesn't do anything to the sound; others believe that black strings sound a bit brighter — or darker…

TIP

Prices

A decent set of nylon strings costs about seven to ten dollars. A really good guitar will benefit from better strings, from ten dollars upwards. It may be worthwhile to try such a set, even if it is just for once. You won't know what you're missing if you don't.

A year or more

Even after a year or more, plain strings can still sound as if they were brand new. Eventually, though, you won't be able to tune them properly anymore and the intonation will be off (see page 53).

Wound strings

Wound strings don't keep their tone that long. Sweat attacks the windings and dirt can easily settle in the grooves between the windings, both resulting in a duller tone. How long that takes may depend on the quality of the strings, on how often you play, how well you look after your strings and, last but not least, on the acidity of your perspiration. The more acidic it is, the faster the sound will deteriorate.

How long

Depending on how much you play, how good your guitar is, and how good you want it to sound, you can change your strings every one or two months, every week, every day, or only when they break. The better your guitar, your playing, and your ears, the sooner you'll hear a loss of brightness and tone. As a starting point: If you put on new strings after a month and you don't hear the difference, you may want to wait a little longer next time. If you hear a difference right away, consider changing strings more often.

Nine or three

Since wound strings lose their tone sooner, it makes sense to replace them more often than your plain ones. For this reason, some brands sell strings in sets of nine, doubling the three wound strings. Others offer strings sets with three wound strings only.

Extra D

The D-string, the thinnest wound string, wears down faster than the other strings. If that sounds like a familiar problem, you may consider buying sets of strings that come with an extra D-string. Strings can be bought one at the time too, but that works out more expensive than buying them per set.

Brands

Some of the main nylon string brands are Aranjuez, Augustine, D'Addario, D'Aquisto, La Bella, GHS, Hannabach, Savarez, and Thomastik-Infeld.

STEEL-STRINGS

Plain steel-strings don't differ that much from one brand to the next. A possible exception is silver steel-strings, which are said to sound a bit more, well, silvery. On steel-string guitars, the third string is usually wound. However, some players prefer a plain G, because it's easier to bend.

Gauges
Steel-strings come in different gauges, from light to heavy. Heavier strings have a higher tension.

Bronze windings
Wound steel-strings are of course available with various types of winding. The silver-plated windings that work so well on nylon strings are rarer on steel-strings. A (80/20) bronze or brass winding, which is more popular, gives steel-strings a loud, bright, and open sound. More copper (e.g., 85%) is said to provide a bit more sustain.

Phosphor bronze
Strings with phosphor bronze windings are a popular alternative. Their sound is often described as bright, full, rich, and warm. The only way to find out what you like is to buy a set and try them on your own guitar; the sound of a set of strings depends on the guitar about as much as the other way around.

Comparing strings
There are lots of other variations, ranging from different windings to strings that combine silk and steel in the core. An effective and inexpensive way to compare strings? Replace one of the wound strings (the fourth or the fifth, preferably) with a string from the brand or series you want to judge. You can also fit a new E of one type of string and a new A of another type. Listen closely, and then replace with a new E of the latter type, and an A of the first type.

TIP

New strings
Of course, there's no point comparing strings unless they're all new. When you compare old and new strings, the new ones will always sound better.

88

This way, you compensate for misleading differences due to string thicknesses and pitches.

Various tensions

Steel-strings come in various gauges. The main differences are shown below.

Lighter gauge strings	Heavier gauge strings
sound 'lighter', edgier, and shorter	sound 'heavier', fatter, and longer
produce less volume	produce more volume
are easier to play	make playing a bit heavier
need to be tuned more often	don't detune as fast
break more easily	last longer
are lower tension	are higher tension

One-hundredth of an inch

String gauges are expressed in fractions of an inch. When guitarists speak about the gauge of a set of strings, they always refer to the first string. In an 010-set, the first string measures 0.010", equaling 0.25 mm. Most steel-string guitar players opt for a set of 012-strings.

Names

Some brands use names to indicate string gauges, often ranging from extra light (010) to heavy (014). The exact names and the gauges they refer to may vary per brand. The same goes for the precise gauges of the other strings in the set.

Gauges

The sixth string is usually around 4.5 times the gauge of the first one: sets range from 010 to 045, and from 012 to 054, for example.

Getting used to it

Most electric guitar players use 010-sets, or even lighter strings. Switching to an acoustic guitar with heavier gauge strings may take some getting used to. You can use 010s on a steel-string guitar, but most instruments will sound better with slightly heavier strings. Heavier strings offer additional volume, increased projection, and a richer, broader tone. You could try a set of 011s before switching to 012, of course.

TIP

Too heavy?
If strings are too heavy for your guitar, they may eventually damage the soundboard or the neck of the instrument. The heaviest sets for steel-string guitars are 014.

Heavier strings, higher tension
The heavier the strings, the more tension they put on your instrument. Replacing your strings with heavier ones may therefore result in a higher action, because of the force they exert at the neck and the top. Of course that higher action can be lowered in turn (see pages 60–62 and 136). If you switch to lighter gauge strings, the lowered action will probably cause string buzz or fret buzz, which can be cured by raising the action.

Caught at the nut
Heavier gauge strings can get caught in the notches of the nut. This make it impossible to tune them properly. The solution is to have the nut replaced or to have the slots or notches adapted.
If you switch to lighter strings, the string slots may be too wide. This allows the strings to move in these notches, resulting in a loss of energy and thus in a loss of tone quality.

Easy
Light gauge strings are easier to play. They typically don't keep their tuning as well as heavier strings. The lower tension can also make you bend strings inadvertently, resulting in out-of-tune chords.

Sweat
How long a set of steel-strings lasts depends on many things. You will have to change them more often than nylon strings: Steel-strings are much more sensitive to sweat, especially if your sweat happens to be very acidic. As with nylon strings, the wound strings

will usually lose their tone and brightness long before the plain ones.

Two weeks, two years

Guitarists who want to keep their sound up to scratch often change their strings every two weeks to two months. There are plenty of players, though, who put on a new set even more frequently. On the other hand, you can easily enjoy one and the same set for over two years. If you use them that long, however, you will be in for a surprise when you install a new set of strings…

Can you hear it?

If you fit new strings after a month and you don't really hear a difference, you could try waiting a little longer the next time. If you do hear the difference, it might be worth changing them sooner next time.

Coating

Some brands make strings with a special coating that reduces the effect of sweat and dirt, extending the string's life expectancy: these strings tend to maintain their original sound for a longer period of time, which compensates for their higher price. The first coated strings were said to sound noticeably different than regular strings, but today's coated strings sound just as good as non-coated ones.

TIP

Prices and brands

A good set of steel-strings costs around seven to ten dollars, but you may find cheaper strings that sound good and hold up well too. Good strings generally sound better, keep sounding good longer and last longer. A few well-known steel-string brands are D'Addario, D'Aquisto, Dean Markley, DR, Ernie Ball, Gibson, GHS, Kyser, Martin, SIT, and Thomastik-Infeld.

91

Cleaning and Changing Strings

To get the best out of your instrument, you'll need to pay some extra attention to your strings — and that doesn't take much time or effort. Keeping them clean and fitting them properly is basically all you need to do. Tuning tips follow in Chapter 9.

To get your strings to last as long as they can, you should take a closer look at your guitar too. First, the smoother the frets are, the longer your strings can last. Rough spots can be smoothed, very carefully, with some ultra-fine steel wool.

Nut and saddle

Second, excessive string wear can be the result of sharp edges at the nut or the saddle. It may pay to check these parts, especially if a certain string keeps breaking in the same place. As before, fine steel wool, or some ultra-fine sandpaper, will usually be all you need to smooth things down.

Elasticity

Even if you never play them, strings gradually lose their elasticity and their sound gets duller. Put on a new set, and the sound will suddenly be bright as can be.

Dust, dirt, grease

Strings also lose their brightness because they are affected by airborne dust, dirt, grease, smoke, and moisture, as well as by whatever your fingers leave on them. Wound strings are especially sensitive to this kind of pollution, because they retain everything so well in their grooves. A guideline: When wound strings start losing their color, they are past their best. They may not break for another year, two years or more, but a new set will dramatically improve the sound of your instrument.

Cleaner and drier

An easy way to keep your strings as dry and clean as possible is to wash your hands and dry them well before playing, and to clean and dry the strings afterwards. Any type of lint-free cloth works well — an old T-shirt or a dishtowel, for instance. Clean the underside of the strings and the fingerboard, as you go along. Simply pull the cloth between the strings and the fingerboard, and run it up and down the neck a couple of times.

String cleaner

If you have particularly sweaty fingers, a special string cleaner may help. These cleaners also remove the dirt from the grooves of your wound strings. They're not expensive — just a couple of dollars buys you a bottle that'll last a long time.

Smoother strings
Other products make your strings feel a little smoother, and they often help to repel dirt as well. Each manufacturer dreams up its own product name, such as Finger-ease or Fast fret. Various string makers apply coatings to their strings for the same purpose, as said on page 91.

> ## Talcum powder
> Rubbing your hands with talcum powder reduces perspiration. Don't use too much, or else the powder will get into the wound strings and muffle them. Washing your hands with pH-neutral soap may limit perspiration too.

TIP

Spare sets
Old strings break more easily than new ones. The more often you change your strings, the less likely it is that they'll give up on you unexpectedly. On the other hand, even a brand new string can break at the first chord. So when you go anywhere with your guitar, always take a spare set with you. Or two, if it's a really important gig.

NEW STRINGS

There are lots of ways to fit new strings. If you do it any of the right ways, your strings will stay in tune as well as they can, and sound good as long as they can. You'll also keep them from damaging your guitar in the process. Here's one of the many right ways to do it, followed by specific tips on replacing nylon strings (page 98) and steel-strings (page 104).

95

Tools

Changing strings is easiest with some tools at hand. The first is a *string winder*, which speeds up the job of loosening and winding the strings. The second is a pair of needle-nose pliers to help you get the ends of the strings out of the tuning machines without cutting your fingers. The third is a wire-cutter to remove the excess length of the strings, before or after putting them on the instrument. Some guitarists also use it to cut the old strings, once the tension is off.

TIPCODE

Tipcode AGTR-008
A string winder helps save time when changing strings.

String winder.

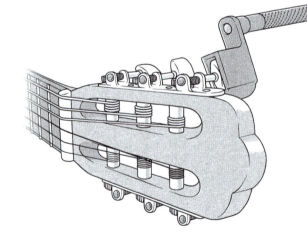

The whole set

If one of your wound strings breaks, you may have to fit a whole new set. A single new one will sound way too bright, compared to the wound strings that you have been playing for a while.

96

Just one

If a plain string breaks, you can usually replace just that one string. Plain strings maintain their sound much longer, so a new one won't usually stand out. That's a good thing, as plain strings tend to break a lot sooner.

TIP

One by one

When putting on a new set, it's best to replace the strings one by one. If you remove all the strings before putting on new ones it'll take your guitar some time to readjust to their tension, which may require a lot of extra tuning.

Tuning to the rest

When adding a new set of strings, most guitarists start with one of the two E-strings and replace the next adjacent one, in ascending or descending order. An advantage of this method is that you can tune each new string to the one next to it — assuming that the guitar is in tune to start with. If not, you'll need a tuning fork or something else to give you a reference pitch, or an electronic tuner (see next chapter).

Elasticity

Strings that lose their elasticity lose their sound too. On the other hand, when they're brand new, strings are way too elastic. Put on a new set and you'll find you have to tune them again and again. Most strings don't sound their best until this initial elasticity has been taken away — which is when they start keeping their tuning better as well.

With steel-strings this only takes a couple of hours. Most types of nylon strings, and especially the plain ones, easily take one or two days to stabilize.

Pre-stretching

This process can be sped up, of course. Slide a finger along the bottom of the strings one by one, and carefully pull them upwards. Retune them. Repeat. And so on, until the tuning is stable.

97

TIPCODE

Tipcode AGTR-009
This Tipcode shows you how to pre-stretch strings. Don't pull too hard!

Cleaning

Some players like to remove all the strings as this allows them to give the fingerboard a good rubdown. There's an alternative way, though, which doesn't require you to take all the strings off at once. First you remove one of the E- strings, creating enough room to take care of that part of the fingerboard. Do the body as well. Then fit the new E-string. Replacing the next strings two by two (A and D; then G and B) will allow you to clean the fingerboard between the other strings. Finish with the other E-string.

On the table

When changing strings it's easiest to lay your guitar flat on a table. A large towel or a piece of foam plastic underneath prevents scratches and keeps it from sliding away. Alternatively, you can put your guitar on your lap.

NYLON STRINGS

Putting new strings on isn't really that difficult — especially once you've done it a couple of times.

Taking your strings off

Start by loosening the first string, until all the tension is off. A string winder will save you a lot of time. When the string is

98

completely slack, it's easy to remove it. Push it back a little at the bridge to give yourself room to undo the knot. Then pull the string out of the bridge, toward the neck. This way, you don't have to pull the entire string through the bridge.

Tipcode AGTR-010
Here's how to untie a nylon a string at the bridge.

TIPCODE

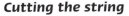

Cutting the string

Some players cut the slackened string in two places; close to the bridge, and just behind the nut, near the tuning machines. The short leftover pieces are easier and safer to remove than an entire string. Other guitarists never cut their strings, as they feel this increases the risk of scratching things.

At the bridge...

Once the old string is off, the new string can be tied to the bridge. The illustration below shows the first step for the first string (high E), the second step for the second string, and so on. This procedure may take some practice at first.

1. Feed the string over the saddle through the appropriate hole in the bridge, until about two inches stick out.

2. Feed this end over the bridge and let it pass under the string.

3. Thread it through the loop. For wound strings just once will do; many players feed the plain strings through the loop three or four times.

4. The last 'knot' should always be behind the bridge, not on top of it.

99

5. Pull the string to tighten the knot.

6. Once the string is tuned, this is how it should look at the bridge.

... and at the tuner

Similar knots should be made at the other end, at the posts of the tuning machines (see the illustrations on page 102). To prevent

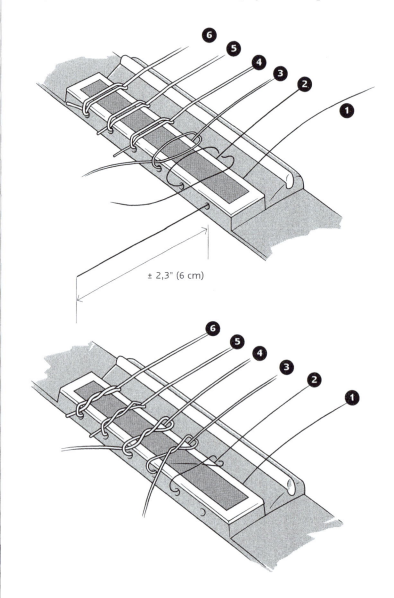

± 2,3" (6 cm)

You can thread the strings around themselves more than once.

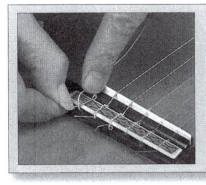

Tipcode AGTR-011
This Tipcode shows you how to
tie a new string to the bridge of a
classical guitar.

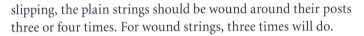

slipping, the plain strings should be wound around their posts
three or four times. For wound strings, three times will do.

1. Feed the string through its post. Leave some slack to allow for
   the required number of windings.

2. Make a loop, as shown in picture 2.

3. Tighten the string, in the direction of the arrow — the knot
   should start to look as shown in picture 3.

4. Once the string has been tuned, the knot will look like the one
   in picture 4.

Tipcode AGTR-012
Tipcode AGRT-012 is the sequel to
AGTR-011, attaching the string to
the tuning post and winding it.

A little tight

To prevent the string from slipping out of its knot at the bridge, you
should keep it under a little tension at all times. When winding the
string, pull it away from the fingerboard with your other hand,

101

1. Through
the hole...

2. Make a
loop...

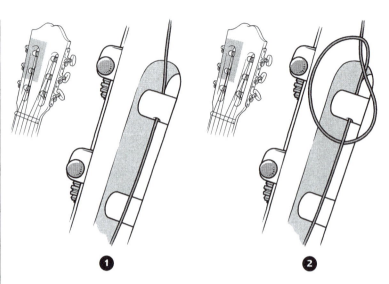

3. The correct
winding
direction for
the post.

4. The
resulting knot.

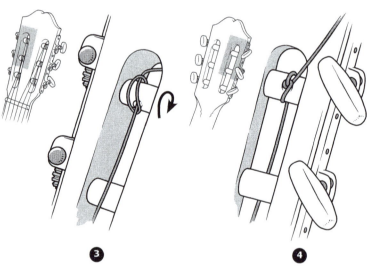

using your index finger to feed it through its slot in the nut. This
also helps make for even windings. The lower illustration on page
107 shows you how.

Inwards and outwards

Both E-strings usually move outwards when winding them, while
the other strings will run in the opposite direction, toward the
middle of the head.

102

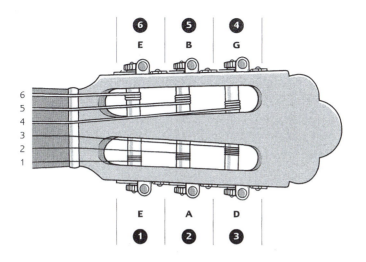

The windings of both E-strings usually run inwards, the others tend to go outwards.

Too long

Most strings are too long. If you attach them to the posts by their ends, you will get so many windings that they get jammed against the inside of the headstock. The solution is to leave just enough slack in the string to make the required number of windings. Four to five inches will do, although this is probably a little on the long side — you can cut off what's left once you're done tuning. Once you are more experienced, you can cut the strings to the desired length before putting them on, so that the excess length doesn't get in your way.

Nylon string tips

- **Loose ends** at the bridge may buzz against the top. Cut them off.

- Instead of pulling the string through the loop at the bridge a couple of times, some players make **a knot at the very end** of the string. Thread the end with the knot through the loop just once, and make sure it ends up at the back of the bridge. Pull the string tight, and it's fixed.

- Some types of nylon strings come with **ball ends**. This little metal ball replaces the knot. Just pull the string through the bridge, starting at the back, and the ball will hold it in place. Most classical guitarists prefer to use the traditional knot, though.

103

STEEL-STRINGS

Most steel-string guitars use pins to attach the strings to the bridge. Others come with slotted bridges, similar to the ones on nylon-string guitars. Again, strings need to be completely unwound before removing or cutting them. Cutting a string that is still under tension can easily cause damage to yourself or your guitar.

Most steel-string guitars use pins to attach the strings to the bridge.

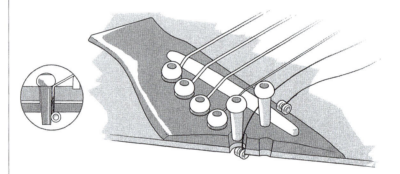

Taking your strings off

Unwind the first string, and take it off the tuner post. At the other end, the string is usually attached with a bridge pin. You can try pulling the pins out with your fingers, you can use a string winder that doubles as a bridge pin puller, or you can get yourself

TIPCODE

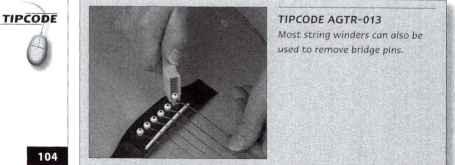

TIPCODE AGTR-013
Most string winders can also be used to remove bridge pins.

a dedicated bridge pin pulling tool. As an alternative you could use a small spoon to lever the pin out of its hole. Other tools may damage your guitar. When the pin is out, you can remove the string.

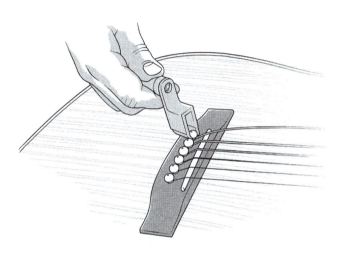

You can easily remove the bridge pins with a string winder.

Attaching the string at the bridge

Now make a slight kink near the ball end of the new string, at the point where it will come out of its hole, once fitted. Then insert the ball end into the hole. Let the string run through the groove in the hole, if there is one. Most bridge pins have grooves too; make sure to insert the pin so that the string runs through it. When inserting the pin, lightly pull the string over the bridge, and keep pulling it as you push the pin down. That's it.

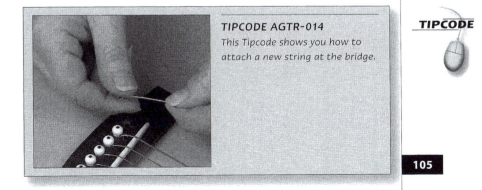

TIPCODE AGTR-014
This Tipcode shows you how to attach a new string at the bridge.

TIPCODE

105

Slotted bridge

If the guitar has a slotted bridge, just pull each string through its appropriate hole. The ball ends will secure the strings. Many roundbacks come with slotted bridges, but you may also find them on other types of guitars. A tip: Go easy when pulling the strings through the bridge in order not to wear them down or cause damage to the guitar or yourself. Strings have sharp ends.

A slotted bridge.

Too long

Like nylon strings, the wound strings should wind around their posts about three times, and the plain ones about four times, to avoid slipping. And just like nylon strings, most steel-strings are too long, so don't attach them to the posts by their ends, or you'll end up with too many windings. You can cut them either after they've been fitted or beforehand, leaving about two inches (5 cm) for the windings.

At the tuner

Now attach the string to the post of the tuner. First turn the appropriate post so that the hole is facing the string.

1. Feed the string through the post. Once is enough.

2. Move it over and around the post once.

3. Start winding the string, making sure it now runs underneath the hole.

4. Lift the string from the fingerboard with your other hand,

106

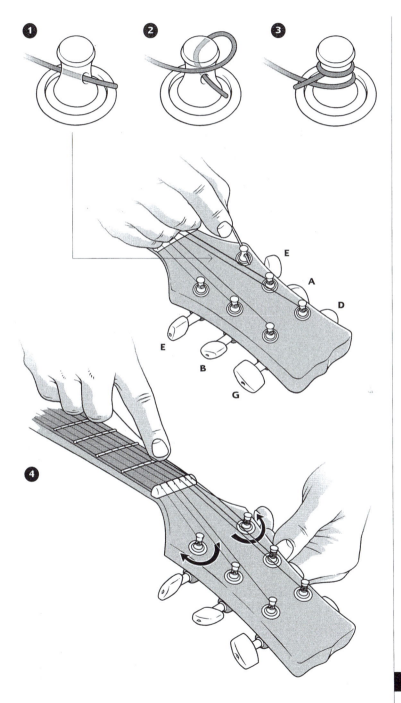

The posts
should turn
in the direction
of the arrows.

keeping it under a little tension. Use your index finger to guide it through the slot in the nut.

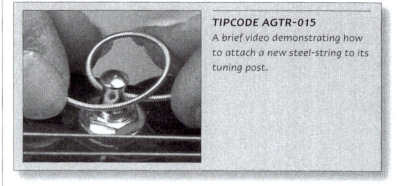

TIPCODE AGTR-015
A brief video demonstrating how to attach a new steel-string to its tuning post.

A better tone

String posts have an hourglass shape, with the narrow waist pushing the windings of each string together. If a string is the right length, the windings will be packed together around the waist of the post only. That'll improve the sound and speed up tuning, and your strings will detune less quickly.

String tips

- Make sure you don't **get any kinks in your strings**; kinks can easily cause breakage. There are two exceptions to this rule. One is described on page 105; the second is that some players use a pair of needle-nose pliers to make a small kink at the other end of each string, so that it hooks around the post.

- You can use the same pair of pliers to **bend the sharp ends** of the strings at the tuning machines down toward the headstock, so you don't prick your fingers.

- It may be hard to tell a thin E-string from a B once all the new strings are out of their bags — so **don't unpack** a string until you're ready to put it on.

- Some manufacturers **print the names** or the numbers of the strings on the bags they're packed in. Others only print the gauges, usually in inches as well as in millimeters.

- Make sure you **never tune your guitar too high or too low**. Strings tend to break and you could damage your guitar if it's tuned too high, while low tunings cause rattles. Besides, a guitar sounds best when it's tuned to its proper pitch, as you'll see in the next chapter.

9

Tuning

Before playing, you have to tune your guitar, or at least check its tuning. Tuning isn't as hard as it may seem at first. You just have to learn how to listen, and you have to know what to listen for and what you're doing. Obviously, you can't learn how to listen just by reading about it — but you'll find everything else in this chapter.

The six guitar strings are tuned to the following pitches:

String **6**	E (the thickest, lowest string)	
String **5**	A	
String **4**	D	
String **3**	G	
String **2**	B	
String **1**	E (the thinnest, highest string)	

Memory aids

Here are three popular memory aids for the guitar's string pitches.

• Even Adam Did Grow Bored Eventually.

• Eating And Drinking Give Brain Energy.

• Even After Death Gamblers Bet Everything.

Too low, too high

A guitar sounds at its best when the strings are tuned exactly to these pitches. If the overall tuning is too low, your guitar may still sound in tune, but the strings will rattle against the frets. If the overall tuning is too high the guitar will be harder to play, you'll run a bigger risk of breaking strings, and you may even bend the neck.

Reference pitch

The standard reference pitch to which most instruments are tuned is A4. This is the note that you will hear if you play the high E-string of a well-tuned guitar at the fifth fret. At this pitch, the string vibrates 440 times per second; it's A=440 Hertz, in official terminology.

By ear

The easiest way to tune your guitar is to use an electronic tuner (page 122). It's also good to learn how to do it by ear, though, so that's where this chapter starts. For this purpose, you need to start with a reference pitch; preferably A=440 (A4).

Piano

A well-tuned piano, or any other keyboard instrument, produces this pitch when you play the A little to the right of the middle of the keyboard (see page 117).

Tuning fork

The same note will sound if you use a tuning fork in A. Just tap this small, thick fork against your knee, say, then — gently — set it against the body of your guitar, or against your ear. That same A can be played back on many electronic metronomes, or you can play Tipcode AGTR-016.

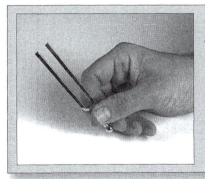

TIPCODE AGTR-016 AND AGTR-017
Tipcode AGTR-016 sounds an A=440, while AGTR-017 demonstrates the use and the sound of an A=440 tuning fork.

TIPCODE

Tuning to A=440

1. First make sure you have an A=440 as your reference pitch.

2. Play the first string (high E), fretting it at the fifth fret. This is supposed to sound that same A. Compare it to your reference A.

3. If the guitar sounds lower, then carefully tighten the string a bit.

4. If it sounds higher, then loosen it carefully.

Two tricks

When you've just started out, it may be hard to hear whether a string sounds too high (*sharp*) or too low (*flat*). Two tricks:

- Always tune up. If a string sounds too high, first loosen it until it sounds obviously too low. Then **go up from there**. This makes it easier to hear what you're doing, and strings keep their tuning better this way.

- **Sing** the pitches you hear. First play and sing the reference pitch, then sing the pitch of the guitar string. Most people will easily learn how to 'sense' if the string sounds higher or lower.

The other strings

Once the high E-string is in tune, you can tune the others to it. Basically all you are doing is continuously comparing one string to the other, as shown in the illustration. Fret one string, and compare it to the next one. Here's how.

- Tune the string you're fretting (on the **solid dot**) to the open string (indicated by an **open dot**).

- The **numbers** of the strings are shown at the bottom.

- The **names** of the strings are shown at the top.

- The **letters** at the very top show you the two notes you hear when you're comparing strings.

Guitar tuning.

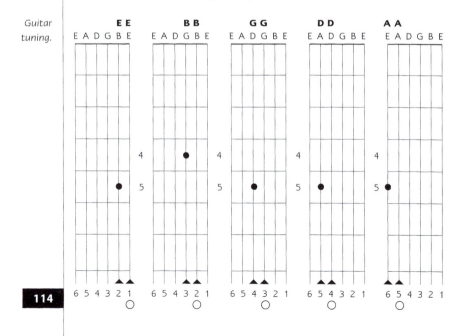

The B, the E, and the rest

Play the B-string at the fifth fret. Compare it to the high E-string you've just tuned.

- Does the B-string sound **too low**? If so, tune it up carefully.

- Does it sound **too high**? First loosen it, till it sounds too low. From there, slowly go up again. Then tune the third string to the second, and so on.

The fifth and fourth frets

Most strings are tuned by playing them at the fifth fret, indicated by the number 5 on the right hand side of the fretboard on the opposite page. The exception is tuning the third string (G) to the second (B), when you play the G-string at the fourth fret.

The other way around

Most guitarists start tuning at the low E, comparing the strings as shown in the illustration on the opposite page, but going from right to left. Being the heaviest string, low E doesn't detune that easily, which also makes it a good starting point if you don't have a reference pitch at hand.

TIPCODE AGTR-018
A basic guitar tuning method: start at low E, and match open strings to stopped strings at the fifth and fourth frets.

TIPCODE

Open strings

A major advantage of tuning from low E is that it allows you to tune open strings while fretting the string you've just tuned. This is easier than tuning fretted strings. After all, a fretted string stops sounding as soon as you release it to change its tension. When tuning open strings, you can adjust the pitch while they're still sounding.

115

Start at the A-string

You can also start tuning at the A-string. One advantage is that you'll hear an A without having to fret a string, which leaves you one hand to hit a tuning fork or piano key. A tip: The open A of this string sounds two octaves lower than the A of a tuning fork, which may make it difficult to compare.

Here's how

First tune the A-string. Now play the A at the fifth fret and tune open D to it. Then tune the other strings, moving from D toward high E.
Once high E is tuned, tune low E to it. Double-check low E by playing the fifth fret and compare that pitch to open A.

Slightly higher or lower

Some orchestras or bands may use a slightly higher or lower tuning, for instance A=442; the higher pitch makes for a slightly brighter overall sound. Most electronic tuners can be calibrated (adapted to other tunings), and tuning forks are available in various pitches.

TIP

Tuning fork in E

For guitarists, there are tuning forks that sound the same high E as the first string (E4).
One advantage of learning to tune to an A, however, is that this is the pitch most bands, orchestras, and other groups tune to.

Twelve-string guitars

Next to each of the four lowest-sounding strings of a twelve-string guitar is a thinner string that sounds exactly one octave higher. The thinner of the two Gs is the highest-sounding guitar string. Both the B and high E-string are accompanied by a second string at the same pitch. These are the notes a twelve-string guitar should be tuned to: E2/E3, A2/A3, D3/D4, G3/G4, B3/B3, E4/E4 (see page 12).

116

The bridge of
a twelve-string
guitar.

Acoustic bass guitars

The tuning of an acoustic bass guitar is similar to that of the four
lowest-sounding strings on a regular guitar — but the instrument
sounds one octave lower (E1, A1, D2, G2).

REFERENCE PITCHES

You can also tune all your strings to the appropriate pitches of a
(well tuned!) piano or another keyboard instrument, or use the
reference pitches of Tipcode AGTR-020 (see page 118).

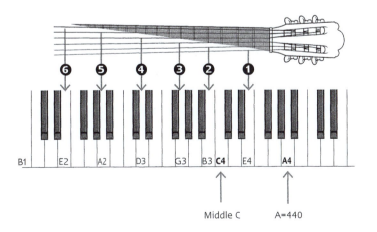

Tuning a
guitar to a
piano.

Middle C   A=440

117

TIPCODE

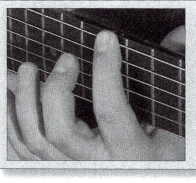

TIPCODE AGTR-020
This Tipccode sounds reference pitches for your guitar strings, starting a low E. Each pitch sounds for eight seconds, and you can play the again and again.

HARMONICS

Using harmonics (see page 54) may both improve and speed up your tuning. When tuning, you will be using the harmonics at the fifth and seventh frets. To really hear them well, touch the string very lightly at the appropriate point with a left-hand finger and strike it firmly, close to the bridge. Playing these harmonics is a bit harder than the ones at the twelfth fret, but it won't take more than a little practice to make them sound right.

Free hand
Tuning with harmonics has two main advantages.

- First, the strings **keep on sounding** once you've released your left hand, so you'll have that one free for tuning.

- Second, it's **easier** to hear when you've reached the right pitch. How? When the pitches of the two strings are almost the same, you'll hear a wavy sound when you play them together. These 'waves' are known as *beats*. Now carefully adjust the string you're tuning. As you get closer, the beats slow down. If you go to far, the beats will start speeding up again. When you're at the right pitch, the beats will be gone: The two strings are in tune with one another, and they sound like one.

Five and seven
The opposite page shows you which strings to compare and which

118

harmonics to play (solid dots). Instead of the open B-string (which is compared to the harmonic at the seventh fret of the low E-string), you can also use the harmonic at the twelfth fret; this will raise the pitch of the B-strings by one octave.

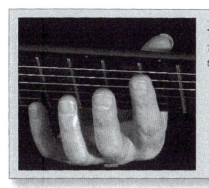

TIPCODE AGTR-019
This Tipcode shows you how to tune a guitar by harmonics.

TIPCODE

The A
Tip: Playing the harmonic at the fifth fret of the A-string produces A4 (A=440).

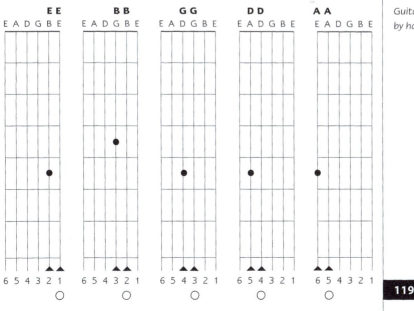

Guitar tuning by harmonics.

PROBLEM? SOLVED!

Unfortunately, the popular tuning method described above is not perfect. As you will hear — if you have a trained ear or good pitch — one or two of your strings may need additional tuning, depending on the chords you're playing. This has to do with the fact that this tuning method uses an interval called a *fifth* (the seventh fret harmonic sounds an octave and a fifth higher than the open string). In order to tune a guitar so that it always sounds in tune, fifths should be tuned a little flat. As this isn't that easy, it's better to go for a tuning method that does not include fifths. Here it is.

The solution

First tune your low E-string, using an electronic tuner.

1. Tune high E to the harmonic at the fifth fret of low E.

2. Tune your D-string: Play the twelfth fret harmonic on low E and compare this pitch to the E on the D-string in second position (at the 2nd fret).

3. Tune your B-string: Play the B-string in third position and compare this pitch (D) to the twelfth fret harmonic on the D-string.

4. Tune your G-string: Play the twelfth fret harmonic on the

TIP

Equal temperament

With this tuning, known as equal temperament, your guitar should sound in tune no matter which chord you're playing or which key you're in. As an alternative, there are some mechanical solutions to solve the same problem, ranging from having the nut replaced and the intonation adjusted according to a special system (e.g., Buzz Feiten), to using two or more curved frets (e.g., Fretwave and True Temperament), or using special nuts (e.g., Earvana).

120

G-string and compare this pitch (G) to the G on high E in third position (at the 3rd fret).

5. Tune your A-string: Play the twelfth fret harmonic on the A-string and compare this pitch to the A on the G-string in second position (at the 2nd fret).

INTERVALS AND CHORDS

Some players prefer to tune their strings by listening to the pitch differences (*intervals*) between the strings, without fretting them or playing harmonics. The interval between the A-string and low E is called a *perfect fourth*.

Amazing Grace
A perfect fourth is what you hear when you sing the first two syllables of *Amazing Grace, Auld Lang Syne, Here Comes the Bride* or *Oh, Christmas Tree*. Sing the first syllable at the pitch that low E gives you; then tune the A-string to the pitch of the second syllable. The same interval is used when going from strings A to D, D to G, and B to high E.

Oh When the Saints
The only interval that's different is the one from G to B; tune it to the first two syllables of *Oh When the Saints Go Marching in*. The name for this interval is a *major third*.

Chords
Alternatively, you can check your guitar's tuning by playing chords and listening if they sound in tune. Preferably do this using one or more chords from the song you're about to play. However, you may find that while one chord sounds great, another one may sound completely off.

One sounds great — but the others
If you tune your guitar so that the first-position E-major chord

121

sounds great, you'll find that that the first-position A-major chord sounds quite a bit less in tune (note the C♯ on the B-string!), and that D-major and C-major are even worse. The solution to this problem is presented on the previous pages.

ELECTRONIC TUNERS

Yet another — and probably the fastest — way to tune your guitar is to use an electronic tuner. This is a small device that shows you whether a string is in tune, too high, or too low.

Microphone and input
Tuners have a built-in microphone that hears the pitch you play. If you have an acoustic-electric guitar, you can plug your instrument cable into the tuner's input, so the tuner reading won't be disturbed by ambient noise or other musicians.

Manual tuners
On the most basic type of tuner, you have to select the instrument you're going to tune (bass or guitar), and then the first string you will tune. Here's how these *manual tuners* work.

1. Select the instrument you're going to tune.

2. Select low E on the tuner.

3. Play low E, and don't play it too hard.

4. If the pointer shows that the string's pitch is too low, tighten the string a little. If it's too high, loosen it a bit.

5. When the pointer hits the middle of the scale, the string is in pitch.

6. Select the next string, tune it — and so on.

7. When all strings have been tuned, check them once more, starting at low E.

Chromatic tuners

Most tuners are *chromatic tuners*, which automatically display the note they 'hear.' This type of tuner requires some very basic knowledge of music theory. If, for example, the tuner displays an F when you play the low E-string, you need to know that this means that the string sounds a half step (semitone) too high.

Faster

Assuming you do know all this, chromatic tuners work a lot faster. Also, they allow you to use non-standard tunings (see page 124).

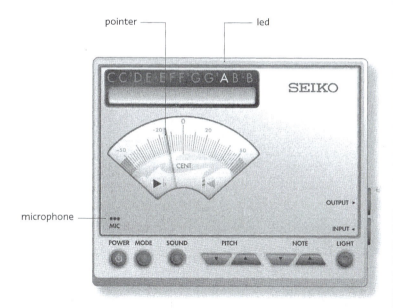

An automatic, chromatic electronic tuner. The A it hears, sounds a little flat.

Numbered notes

Chromatic tuners often display the numbered note names (e.g., low E is E2; see page 12). Manual tuners display the string numbers instead. In that case, that same low E-string is now indicated as 6E, the sixth string of the instrument. Confusing, but true.

123

Clip tuners

Tuning an acoustic guitar on a noisy stage is quite hard, and a tuner may hear much more sounds than the pitch of the string you're playing. A vibrational tuner solves this problem effectively. You simply clip the tuner on the headstock of your guitar, where it registers the vibrations of the strings rather than their sound: Ambient noise is no longer a problem.

Electronic tuner tips

Chromatic tuners are available from about twenty to a hundred dollars and more.

- Better tuners **respond faster** and may hold the reading a little longer.

- Many good tuners also generate **reference pitches** (three or more octaves). The ones that do often have a separate headphone output.

- Also check how well the tuner can be read on a **dark stage** (some have a backlit display).

- Tuners with a mechanical pointer are usually **slower** and use more energy than the ones with an LCD pointer. LED pointers (small 'lights') are easy to read on dark stages.

- Some tuners double as a **metronome** (see page 30).

- An **Auto Power Off** feature turns the tuner off after a while, saving expensive batteries.

TIP

Check

Always check your tuning after you've tuned to an electronic tuner, using any of the methods mentioned above — or all of them.

NON-STANDARD TUNINGS

There are all kinds of different tunings you can use on your guitar — an open tuning for instance, which involves tuning the strings to a specific chord. Also, you can raise the entire pitch of the guitar by using a capo, making all the strings sound any number of half steps (half tones or semitones) higher.

Open tuning

Open tunings are very popular. An open tuning simply means that you tune your strings to sound a chord when you play them all 'open', i.e., without fretting them. If, for example, you tune to D, G, D, G, B, and D (low to high), strumming the *open* strings will sound a G-major chord. A song that consists of major chords only, can now be played using no more than your left index finger. Place it over all six strings (*barre*) and simply slide from chord to chord.

Slide

You can also do so with a *slide*. A slide is a tube, usually made out of metal, which you slip over one of your left-hand fingers and slide over the strings. Country and blues guitarists often use this technique. Originally, *bottle necks* were used for slides, and glass slides are still available.

Fingerpicking

The G-major tuning is often used, both for slide playing and for fingerpicking. Fingerpickers also like D, A, D, G, A, D or a similar tuning with the G tuned down to F-sharp or E.

Personal

Some guitarists use their own personal tunings. The open tuning E, A, C♯, E, A, E (A-major), for example, was made famous by

> **Tip**
>
> If an alternative tuning requires you to tune a string way up or down, you may consider using a different string gauge.

125

Bonnie Raitt. C, G, D, A, E, G and E, A, D, G, C F are two tunings used by Robert Fripp (Brian Eno, King Crimson).

A capo

For some songs it may be useful to be able to raise the entire tuning of your guitar by any number of half steps. A capo does that for you: Simply put it in the position where you need it, close to the fret, as you would your fingers (see page 61).

TIPCODE

TIPCODE AGTR-021
A capo allows you to raise the pitch of your instrument by one or more half steps.

Buying a capo

There are different capos for classical guitars and steel-string guitars, as their fingerboards don't have the same shape (see page 57–58). You can get a wide variety of capos for both types of guitars, from very basic models that use a rubber band to clever designs that can be put on and taken off with one hand, or even rolled up and down the neck. Special capos for twelve-string guitars are also available. *Tip:* Some capos tend to make one or both E-strings buzz.

FINAL GUITAR TUNING TIPS

• A set of **pitch pipes** can be used too. They're as cheap as they are portable, but they tend to go out of tune rather quickly.

- **Strings detune faster** when they're brand new (be patient, or pre-stretch them: see page 97) or when they slip (put them on right; see pages 98–109).

- If **the slots in the nut** aren't wide enough for the string gauges you're using, tuning may be difficult. A temporary solution is to repeatedly press the string right behind the nut while tuning it. Tune, press, listen, tune... A better solution is to have the nut replaced or adjusted.

- Tuning can be made even smoother if you sprinkle some graphite (available at your hardware store) in the string slots, rub a **pencil's point** in them, or use a drop of Teflon lubricant.

10

Picks and Nails

Most steel-string guitarists use a pick. Classical
guitarists pluck the strings with their fingertips and
their nails. Fingerpickers do the same, unless they're
using special fingerpicks. Flamenco guitarists mainly use
their nails.

You can make any guitar sound more powerful, warmer, brighter, rounder, meaner, or smoother, by striking the strings in different positions — close to the bridge or the neck — or by muffling them slightly with the side of your hand. What you use to strike the strings with has a big influence on the sound too. A hard pick yields a different sound than a fleshy fingertip, for instance.

PICKS

Almost every music store offers loads of picks to choose from, in all sorts of shapes, weights, sizes, and colors. Bright-colored picks are easier to find once you've dropped them. Apart from that, your choice mainly depends on what you play, how you play, and what suits you best.

Large or small
Most picks are quite small. Larger models are often used by country & western guitarists, bass players, 12-string players, and guitarists who want to have a little extra grip on things.

Heavy or light
Each brand makes picks in different weights. A light one may be as thin as less than 0.5 mm). Regular heavy picks are more than twice as thick, and there are much thicker ones too.

- Most players use a relatively **light pick** for strumming. A slightly heavier pick will help to increase volume and projection.

- **Heavier picks** make for a heavier, thicker, full-bodied sound, both requiring and providing more precision. Better players typically use heavier — and thus harder — picks, which also help increase speed.

Hard or soft
Of course there are light picks that are quite hard, and heavy ones that feel pretty soft and flexible. Just try out a bunch — they cost next to nothing, with the exception of special products such as

130

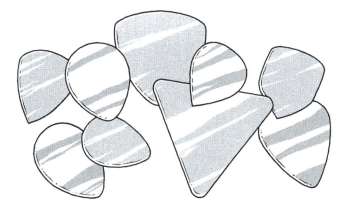

... in all sorts of shapes, weights, sizes...

handmade wooden, bone or (buffalo) horn picks. Also ask other guitarists what they use.

Which pick?

For chord playing, most guitarists use soft picks. They're easy to play and make for an even sound. Solo guitarists often prefer smaller, harder picks. Need something really aggressive? Try a metal pick.

Which shape?

The shape of the pick affects the sound in a predictable way: a sharp point will promote a pointed attack, while a rounded shape will make for a rounder tone.

Sweaty fingers

Sweaty fingers? Buy a pick with an anti-skid profile (raised lettering, for example), or buy a celluloid one, as this material is less slippery. Also available are picks with cork patches or perforations.

TIP

Over your fingers

For fingerpicking there are special picks that you slide over your fingers. Banjo players use them too.

131

Some thumbpicks and fingerpicks.

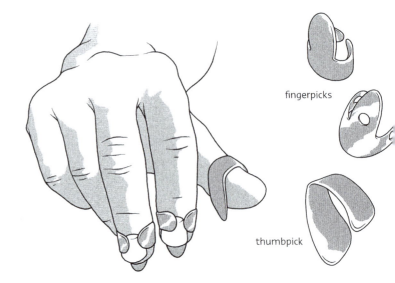

fingerpicks

thumbpick

Tips

- Check picks for **rough edges**, as they will scrape your strings. Some fine sandpaper or a nail file is all you need to smoothen them up a little.

- Want to play chords and use a pick but your guitar has no **pickguard**? Have one installed, so you won't scratch the varnish off the body.

- Picks are available in a **wide variety of materials**, ranging from various types of plastics to metal, felt, and stone. Many players regret that tortoise shell picks are no longer available: They were extremely durable and made for a beautiful tone.

NAILS

Flamenco guitarists mainly use their nails, while classical guitarists and fingerpickers may use both their nails and their fingertips. Nails that are too short make for a dull sound, and worn down or split nails don't sound good and may even get caught behind the strings. How do you keep your nails in good shape?

132

Water and gloves

Water makes your nails go soft. Soapy water is even worse. Try to wear household gloves when you do the dishes or wash your car.

Nail care

For the best results, your nails need to be a certain length and shape. Which length and which shape works best for you depends on more factors than can be dealt with here. Four examples: how hard your nails are, how thick they are, how rounded they are, and how you play. Ask your teacher for advice, experiment, and talk to other guitar players. The same goes for many other nail-related questions.

Textures

To smooth down your nails, you can get files with various textures. Start with a coarse texture, and use the finest for the final step, polishing the tip of each nail to a high gloss.

Good food

A well-balanced diet is important for your nails. White (weak) spots, nails that grow too slowly, or weak nails, to mention a few examples, can all be due to certain food deficiencies. Problems with your nails? Consult a doctor or a dietician.

TIP

Nail strengthener

Nails that tear or peel easily may be remedied by using a nail strengthener, available from drugstores. Carefully apply some every couple of weeks until your nails are as hard as you need them to be. From then on just use as much as you need to keep them that way. A warning: If your nails are too hard, they'll break easily — so use strengtheners and similar products in moderation, and keep an eye on your nails.

Personal remedies

Some players combine nail strengthener with nail oil. Others strictly advise against nail strengthener, swearing instead by the

133

use of laurel balm applied daily to cuticles. In other words, there are as many remedies and methods as there are guitarists.

Artificial nails

What if nail strengtheners and other solutions don't do the trick? You could consider artificial nails. Most are not designed for guitar playing, though. Artificial nails used for playing should be strong, and they should very closely follow the shape of your own nails. Some players even make their own artificial nails, in the exact shape they need.

11

Maintenance and Cleaning

Adjusting and repairing a guitar should be left to a specialized technician. That leaves you to keep your guitar clean and in good working order, both at home and on the road. Here's what you can do yourself, plus some of the things that are best left to a professional.

A crack in the top, a loose brace, a buzzing sound that you can't trace, a bridge that comes loose... All good reasons to go see a technician. But there's more.

Action

The action of your guitar will probably need adjusting when you change to heavier or lighter strings: heavier strings exert more tension, often raising the action, and vice versa. The solution is to either lower or replace the saddle or the nut, or both. Most steel-string guitars have an adjustable truss rod that can be used to change the action. Adjusting this rod is a job best left to a technician, and it's safest to visit one for any other job that requires tools other than the ones you need to change your strings.

CLEANING

A clean guitar will last longer, it'll be easier to play, and it'll be worth more if you want to trade it in for a better one. Nobody really seems to agree on the best way to clean guitars: There is no 'best way,' but there are plenty of tips.

Strings

Cleaning strings has been dealt with in Chapter 8. Please note that most guitar cleaners should be kept away from strings; what's good for the varnish may not be so good for your strings.

The fingerboard

When wiping your strings after playing, you can easily clean the fingerboard as well, as described on page 94. If you always do that, you probably won't need to use any of the special fingerboard cleaners that are available. A soft toothbrush may be used to clean the fingerboard where it meets the frets and the nut. Many players treat their fingerboard with a little fingerboard oil or fretboard conditioner, say once a year, to keep it smooth and clean.

Cleansers

Some guitarists use steel wool, liquid, or any other household products to clean dirty fingerboards. These experiments are never risk-free. Steel wool can easily damage more than it cleans, and household detergents may be too abrasive or leave residues. The most important advice? Ask a technician for advice, and bring along your guitar when you do. That way you can also choose to have it cleaned for you.

The body
Cleaning the body is mainly a matter of lightly and frequently wiping it with a dry or slightly moist lint-free cloth.

Varnish, varnish, and varnish
Use a dedicated guitar cleaner if you are aiming to seriously clean the body, remove fingerprints and stains, and possibly even restore the finish to its original luster. Please note that special finishes may require special cleaners. What's good for one finish, another can't take. Bodies that are finished with oil or wax also require their 'own' cleaners. Once again, when in doubt, ask your technician for advice, and if necessary bring your guitar along.

Special cleaners
Special guitar cleaners, with names such as *guitar polish*, *guitar juice* or *guitar gloss*, work fine on most instruments. Some products may be meant to clean only the woodwork, while others are supposed to restore its original luster too. Read the instructions beforehand, then pick one, and read the instructions once more before applying it.

TIP

Furniture cleaners
Some guitarists — experienced ones too — happily use the very furniture cleaners that others have warned against for years. A common objection to these cleaners is that they may build up a greasy residue on the instrument's surface. Guitar cleaners are not supposed to do that. Yes, special guitar cleaners cost a lot more, but they last a long time too, so you might consider how much you'll actually save by using household products.

137

Brands

Guitar cleaners are supplied by companies such as D'Andrea, Dunlop, Number One, GHS, and Kyser. Some guitar manufacturers have their own cleaners, which are often made by a dedicated company.

Tuning machines

Open tuning machines can be lubricated with light machine oil. Twice a year will do, using a tiny, tiny drop only. Don't apply the oil directly, but rather dip a match in the oil, then apply it to the tuner. Turn it a couple of times, and you're done. As an alternative you may use some silicone-based slot spray. Again, a tiny bit will do for months. Sealed tuning machines are self-lubricating.

Dust

A small brush, or a toothbrush as mentioned earlier, will come in handy when removing dust and dirt from the smallest corners and edges. A vacuum cleaner's smallest fitting can be used to remove dust from within the body. Preferably do that when replacing strings; that will give you more room to get inside.

DRY AIR

When air humidity is high, wood tends to expand. When the air gets too dry, it'll shrink. Sudden humidity changes and low air humidity are among a guitar's worst enemies. If the wood gets too dry, the braces or the bridge may come loose, the top may crack, or frets (which don't shrink) may jut out from the sides of the neck (which does). And there's more that may go wrong, so do take care.

Hygrometers

When it comes to air humidity, guitars and people are quite similar: Both like it to be around 50% to 60%. You can check the level of air humidity with a hygrometer, available for some fifteen dollars or more.

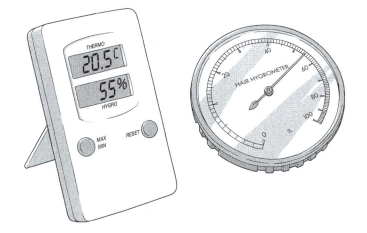

A digital hygrometer and a traditional hair hygrometer.

Guitar humidifiers

Central heating and air conditioning are two of the main causes of dry air, so take extra care if your house has either, or both. There are all kinds of small affordable humidifiers that can be used inside the guitar case; some are designed to be installed in the soundhole of the instrument. Also, there are cases that have built-in humidifiers, or even a hygrometer and a thermometer.

No refill

Traditional humidifiers need a water refill from time to time. Modern versions, which can both emit and absorb moisture, maintain the required relative humidity without refills.

All-around solutions

If air humidity is very low in your house, both your guitar and yourself may benefit from a central humidifier (if your heating system allows for one) or a portable one. Some examples of the latter are steam humidifiers (affordable, fast, but may be noisy) and cold humidifier systems which are quieter but more expensive, take longer to work, and need frequent maintenance (cleaning, filling, and so on).

Time to adjust

If it's extremely cold outside, and you take your instrument someplace where it's warm, or vice versa, allow your guitar some

139

time to adjust to the new surroundings before unpacking it. Take it out after fifteen minutes, or as much longer as you can. The more gradually things change, the better your instrument will like it.

TIP

Heaters and windows

Some don'ts: Never store your guitar in direct sunlight, near heaters or fireplaces, or anywhere else where it may get too hot or too cold. If you hang it from a wall at home, preferably choose an inside wall.

Sounds a little excessive? According to experts, about ninety percent of all acoustic guitar problems are related to changes in air humidity or temperature.

Solid tops
Guitars with laminated tops are less sensitive to all of the above than guitars with solid tops — but take care with those as well.

CASES AND BAGS

Cases and gig bags offer protection against damage on the road, but they're also useful in keeping airborne dust and dirt from your instrument when you don't play.

Gig bags
Basic *gig bags* are available for as little as twenty dollars or less, while leather models may cost as much as three hundred. More money buys you a more effective (not necessarily meaning thicker!) shock-absorbent padding, a tougher, water resistant exterior, reliable zippers that won't scratch your instrument, wider, more comfortable adjustable shoulder straps and backpack straps, and perhaps details such as a recessed area for the vulnerable strap pin. Some bags (and cases) offer extra support and stabilization for the — vulnerable — neck of the instrument.

Extra pockets

Most gig bags have extra pockets for spare strings, picks, an electronic tuner, cables, sheet music, or even an instrument stand or a music stand. Gig bags are less expensive, lighter, and easier to carry than most *hard-shell* cases, but a good hard-shell case offers better protection.

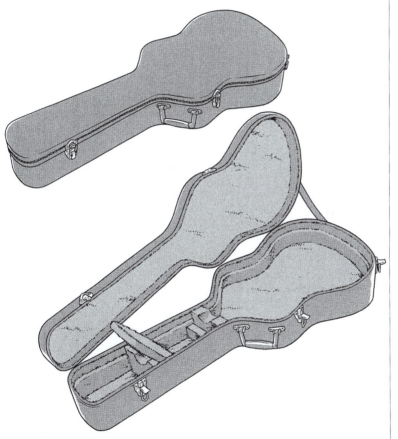

A hard-shell case.

Hard-shell cases

Cases come in different qualities too, starting at as little as forty dollars for a case with a chipboard shell. Cases with plywood or molded plastic shells are stronger, but more expensive. A hard-shell case needs to perfectly fit your instrument. Top quality cases may cost four hundred dollars.

141

Form-fitting or rectangular

Form-fitting cases usually offer less room for accessories than rectangular models, but most have at least one padded accessory compartment. The instrument is protected against scratches by a soft (usually plush or plush cotton) lining. Some cases have special features such as a support channel for the neck, or a built-in hygrometer and humidifier. Well-designed models have one or more thoroughly attached handles at strategic places.

Remove your strap

Always remove the strap from your instrument before putting it in its case or bag. One of the reasons to do so is that some types of strap material may damage your finish.

GUITAR STANDS

Intermission? Put your instrument in a good stand, rather than leaning it against a wall, your amp, or a piece of furniture.

Foldable guitar stand.

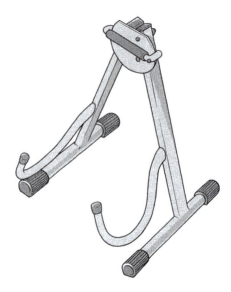

Small or big

Some stands have been designed to fit a large accessory pocket, when folded up. Others don't fold up that compactly, but are designed for maximum stability. If you use more than one instrument, you can get yourself a multi-guitar stand; some cases even double as one.

Cover the cushions

The padded arms and back rest of a guitar stand can damage some natural types of finish (e.g., nitro-cellulose). To prevent this, simply cover the pads with cotton cloth.

Neck support

Not all stands offer a separate neck support. The ones that do may have a security strap or a locking system for extra safety. On some stands, the neck support locks automatically (e.g., Auto Grab).

U-shape

Another product that helps prevent your guitar from falling over is a u-shaped plastic device that can plugged into a spare input or the headphone jack of your amp. There are similar products that can be stuck to a chair, an amp or a table, for instance.

ON THE ROAD

Taking your guitar on the road? Here are a few tips.

- Never leave your stuff in a car **unattended**.

- One of the worst places for a guitar, on the road, is the back shelf of a car, in plain view and direct sunlight. The best place, in a car? **On the back seat**, where it's not as cold (or as hot) as in the trunk.

- Flying? Then it's best to carry your instrument as **carry-on luggage**, if that's allowed.

- If your guitar has a **serial number**, you'll probably find it on the back of the head, or on the label or somewhere else inside the

143

body. Jot it down, preferably before your instrument is stolen or lost. There's room to do so on page 226.

- Consider **insuring your instrument**, especially if you're taking it on the road — which includes visiting your teacher. Musical instruments fall under the 'valuables' insurance category. A regular homeowner insurance policy will not cover all possible damage, whether it occurs at home, on the road, in the studio, or onstage.

12

History

As string instruments have been around for thousands of years, the guitar has many ancestors. There are almost as many stories on how one instrument led to another — and they're often contradictory. In this chapter you'll find some of the highlights; there are plenty of books around that can fill in the details.

In the days when supper was still something you hunted, humans discovered that shooting an arrow produces a tone, due to the vibration of the string. Many years later, someone found a way to amplify that sound by attaching a gourd to the bow. And so the first forefather of the guitar was born.

Seventeenth-century guitar with five pairs of strings.

Luthier

Numerous variations on the first string instruments have appeared all around the world, eventually leading to the modern-day guitar. One of its best-known ancestors is the lute (see page 158), which explains why guitar makers are still referred to as luthiers. The first instruments to resemble today's guitar emerged in the sixteenth century. They often had five single or double strings, lacking a low E.

Antonio de Torres Jurado

Some time between 1850 and 1860 the Spaniard Antonio de Torres Jurado built the instrument on which today's classical guitar is based. Torres, as he's usually referred to, combined a slightly bigger body with an improved bracing pattern (fan-bracing) and the current scale, which turned out to be a great recipe. Though his name is still remembered, Torres never really profited from his valuable contributions to the history of the guitar; poverty even forced him to accept other kinds of jobs from time to time… He died in 1892, at the age of 75.

Before nylon

Classical or Spanish guitars have been referred to as 'nylon-string guitars' only since the 1950s, when these strings were introduced.

Before then, gut was used for the plain strings, while the wound strings had a silk core. Nylon strings quickly took over from gut, as they sound brighter and louder, they are easier to play as well as more reliable and consistent, and their tuning doesn't drop when air humidity goes up.

THE STEEL-STRING GUITAR

While Torres was working on the classical guitar in Spain, Christian Friedrich Martin was designing the forerunner of today's steel-string guitar in the US.

America
The German luthier Martin (1796–1867) moved to America around the age of thirty-seven. In 1839 he settled in Pennsylvania. About ten years later he developed the X-bracing that is still used for most steel-string guitars.

Not for steel
Contrary to what you may think, Martin didn't come up with X-bracing to deal with the high tension of steel-strings; they weren't

Arch-top guitar with a pickup.

introduced until the late nineteenth century. The Dreadnought, first made by the Martin company for a brand by the name of Oliver Ditson, made its debut in 1916. The name Dreadnought (meaning 'fear nothing') is taken from a large British battleship.

Archtops

In the 1930s, arch-top guitars, which were predominantly used by jazz players, became increasingly popular. The archtop doesn't seem to have had a single inventor, though the name of luthier Orville Gibson, founder of the Gibson company, is often mentioned. The (electric) archtop or hollow-body guitar is still favored by most jazz guitarists.

Acoustic-electric

The acoustic-electric guitar gained worldwide acceptance in the early 1980s, Ovation being the first company to equip guitars with built-in piezo pickups on a large scale.

13

The Family

The acoustic guitar belongs to the huge family of
string instruments. In this chapter you'll meet some
of its closer family members only, all belonging to the
category of fretted instruments — some common, some
rare.

Sizes
As stated in Chapter 5, nylon-string guitars are available in various sizes. Apart from the children's and ladies' sizes mentioned in that chapter, there are quite a few other nylon-string fretted instruments.

Higher
The *requinto*, the main instrument used by Mexican mariachi bands, is just one example of a smaller professional guitar. Another is the *alt* or *alto*, with a 21" scale (54 cm). Most smaller guitars are tuned higher — a minor third, a fourth, or even a fifth higher, depending on the exact size and use of the guitar.

Lower
Baritone guitars are slightly larger, and they're tuned a bit lower than 'regular' guitars. The instrument is usually tuned a fourth below a regular guitar (B, E, A, D, F♯, B), but some tune it a fifth lower (A, D, G, C, E, A), or no more than three half steps or semitones (C♯, F♯, B, E, G♯, C♯).

Small steel-strings
There are also really small steel-string models, which are tuned a bit higher. One example is the *terz guitar*. This short-scale instrument is usually tuned a minor third higher (G, C, F, B-flat, D, G).

More strings
Most guitars have six strings, but you can get more too, the best known example being the twelve-string guitar (pages 68–69). These are usually steel-strung instruments, but there are nylon-string models as well. Guitars with more than six single strings are even rarer, but you may come across instruments with a seventh string, usually tuned to low-A or B, and guitars with ten or eleven single strings.

Double-neck
Electric guitars with two necks aren't that exceptional, but acoustic double-necks are quite rare. The one shown here is a design that has been used by Jimmy Page (Led Zeppelin) and Richie Sambora (Bon Jovi).

Acoustic-
electric
double-neck
(Ovation).

Certain styles
Some types of guitars are used mainly in certain styles of music,
such as the Selmer and Maccaferri models for flamenco music.

Flamenco
The flamenco guitar is a nylon-string instrument with a body
that's often slightly smaller than that of a classical guitar.
Combined with a thin top and the use of particular types of wood,
this makes for the penetrating, fierce sound of these instruments.
Rather than using regular tuning machines, flamenco players
often prefer wooden tuning pegs, similar to those of a violin. One
or two transparent *golpeadores* protect the top against the nails of
the player.

Maccaferri
Around 1930, the Italian guitarist Mario Maccaferri introduced
a classical guitar with a cutaway, a large D-shaped soundhole,
and an extra sound chamber, mounted inside the body. The
design was rather too revolutionary for classical players, but jazz
guitarist Django Reinhardt liked it very much — and to this day
you'll find this type of guitar in many gypsy jazz bands. These
slotted-head (!) instruments have steel-strings that are attached to
a tailpiece, rather than to the bridge. The French Selmer company
built Maccaferri guitars for a few years before introducing its own
model with a smaller, oval soundhole and no second chamber.

151

*Maccaferri
guitar
(Van Oosterhout).*

Columbus

The requinto or *guitarrico* was one of the instruments that was
developed in South and Central America, after Columbus had
introduced the guitar to the New World. Some other examples
are the five-string *quinto*, the four-string *cuatro* or *quarto*, and the
ukelele — and there are many more.

Resonator

An eye-catching steel-string variation is the resonator, which
usually has a metal body and a top that contains one or more
resonators — metal discs that amplify and color the sound. This
type of guitar, developed in the US in the 1920s and known for
its metallic tone — naturally — is often used by blues musicians,
played with finger picks and a slide. There are basses and acoustic-

electric models too. Some call these guitars Dobro's, which is the brand name that was used by the brothers Ed and Rudy Dopyera (Dopyera Brothers). Another well-known brand name is National.

Resonator guitar.

Travel guitars

Some guitars are not designed for a specific sound, but with a particular purpose in mind. Portability, for instance. Two of the many examples of these so-called travel guitars are the Baby Taylor, featuring a short scale and a removable neck, and the Martin Backpacker, available with nylon or steel-strings. Other variations include fully collapsible instruments with a metal frame, rather than a traditional body.

A travel guitar: the Backpacker (Martin).

153

ELECTRIC GUITARS

The main difference between electric and acoustic guitars is that the electric ones need amplification: Instead of a hollow soundbox, which acoustically amplifies the sound, most electric guitars have a *solid body* — and that's what these guitars are known as.

Pickups

Most solid-body guitars have two or three pickups, mounted between the bridge and the neck. A switch usually allows the

The two best-known electric guitars: a Stratocaster (Fender) with three single-coil pickups, and a Les Paul (Gibson) with two humbuckers.

154

choice of any combination of these pickups. The two main types of pickup are single-coils and humbuckers, the latter yielding a warmer, rounder, or fatter sound with less hum (hence its name). Some guitars have humbuckers or single-coil pickups only; others combine the two.

If a guitar has two identical pickups, the one near the bridge delivers a brighter sound than the one near the neck — comparable to what happens if you play an acoustic guitar near the bridge, or the neck.

Hollow-body

Jazz and blues guitarists usually play arch-top guitars fitted with one or, more commonly, two magnetic pickups. These guitars are often referred to as *hollowbodies*.

Alternate names

Some also call them *full-body guitars*, because they have deep bodies, and others refer to them as *semi-acoustic guitars*. Similar instruments with a shallower body (some two to three inches) are known as *slim-line* or *thin-line guitars*.

Electric guitars

Want to learn about electric guitars and bass guitars? Check out *Tipbook Electric Guitar and Bass Guitar* (see page 232).

ACOUSTIC OR ELECTRIC

Many guitars are neither fully electric nor completely acoustic. An example would be a 'classic electric' guitar with a shallow, almost solid body (sometimes referred to as a *semi-solid*) and a piezo pickup; or an instrument that plays like an electric guitar yet has a very acoustic sound, or an acoustic-electric with a rather shallow body in the shape of a well-known solidbody... The names of such guitars often indicate what they're about: Classic Electric (Gibson), Acousticaster (Godin), Stratacoustic (Fender), and Ampli-Coustic (Renaissance) are just some examples.

Electric feel,
acoustic sound
(Godin).

MODELING AND MORE

A more recent addition to the market is a type of guitar that can sound both like an electric guitar and an acoustic instrument, using a technology known as *modeling*. Modeling can be used to digitally recreate the sound of any type of instrument. Modeling guitars may have more then twenty different guitar sounds on board, ranging from steel-strings and nylon-string guitars with six or twelve strings to electric guitars and ethnic string instruments.

Microphone
These instruments typically offer all kinds of 'acoustic' adjustments. For example, you may be able to position a virtual

TIP

Open tunings

On a modeling guitar, switching to an open tuning is a matter of pushing the right button. The string tuning doesn't change, but the instrument will sound the required pitches anyway (unless you play it acoustically, of course). Likewise, it's possible to make the bass strings sound a octave lower, while your treble strings keep their regular tuning. A capo is useless: you can virtually tune your guitar as high as you like.

156

microphone: Moving it closer to the soundhole will increase the sound your pick makes when it hits the strings.

MIDI and USB

A growing number of electric and acoustic-electric guitars can be directly plugged into a (guitar) synthesizer, a computer or any other type of digital equipment, using a MIDI interface. MIDI stands for Musical Instrument Digital Interface. A USB connector is not uncommon either, and there are guitar cables with a built in interface, allowing you to plug your acoustic-electric instrument directly into a USB port on your computer.

STEEL GUITARS

The lap steel guitar is played strings facing up, either on the player's lap (*lap steel*) or on a stool. The steel-strings are played with a thumb pick and fingerpicks. A slide or *steel* is used to stop the strings.

The high action of steel-string guitars (say half an inch) and the use of the slide make frets redundant. The positions are indicated with stripes or other markers.

Square neck resonator

Regular steel-string guitars — especially resonators — are sometimes used for lap steel playing, typically featuring a raised action and a square neck.

Pedal steel

A pedal steel is mounted on a frame. These instruments often have two or three necks, with eight, ten, twelve or more strings per neck. The tuning of the instrument can be changed via pedals and knee levers. The right foot operates an expression pedal (volume).

Styles

Lap and pedal steel guitars are mainly used in music from Hawaii, country, and bluegrass, as well as in other styles of music.

157

MORE FRETTED INSTRUMENTS

There are lots of other fretted instruments, usually with four or more strings. A short introduction, which is by no means complete.

Lute
You don't see too many lutes around today. This ancestor of the guitar has a pear-shaped body, a rounded back, and sides made of wooden strips, a short, wide neck, wooden tuning pegs, and a very intimate, mellow sound.

Mandolin
The original mandolin, with an even shorter neck, is clearly related to the lute. Today most mandolins look quite different, as the illustration shows: They still have a short neck, but they have arched tops (though flat-top models are available too) and, often, a flat back. The four pairs of strings are tuned to G, D, A, and E, from high to low. The two G-strings have the same pitch as the G on a guitar. Some variations on the mandolin are the *mandola*, the twelve-string *mandriola*, and the *mandocello*.

Mandolin.

Banjo
The *banjo* has a round body and a skin that acts as the top. It has four or five strings and a very short, percussive sound, and is

played with finger picks. Five-string banjos, like the mandolin, are mainly used in bluegrass and country, while the four-string is often played in folk and Dixieland bands.

A five-string banjo.

Saz, balalaika, and bouzouki

Many cultures have their own string instruments. Just a few of the hundreds of different variations are the Turkish *saz-baglama*, usually known as the *saz*, with two sets of two and one set of three strings, adjustable frets, a long neck and a relatively small body; the somewhat similar looking Greek four-course (eight strings in four pairs) *bouzouki*; the long-necked Russian *balalaika* with its triangular body; and the Bulgarian *tambura* with a very shallow, pear-shaped body and four double strings.

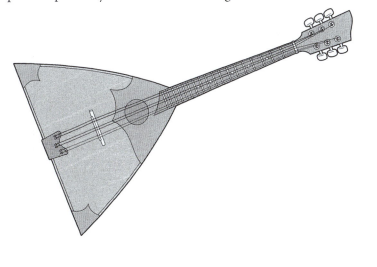

A balalaika, from Russia.

159

14

How They're Made

Guitars are made in large plants and small workshops.
Though production processes may differ in many ways,
the basic principles of guitar construction are quite
straightforward.

There are guitar factories where twenty workers produce something like twenty thousand guitars per year. On the other hand, there are luthiers who make one every two months. One major difference? The luthier will carefully hand-pick each and every part, matching them for sound and color — which is unlikely to happen in a factory setting.

TIPCODE

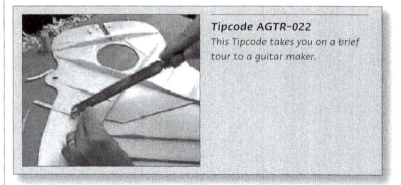

Tipcode AGTR-022
This Tipcode takes you on a brief tour to a guitar maker.

Bookmatched tops and backs

Solid tops are made by splitting a solid piece of wood, resulting in two planks that are the mirror image of each other. Glued together they make a bookmatched top. The same technique is sometimes used for backs, as well as for the outer ply of laminated tops.

A bookmatched top.

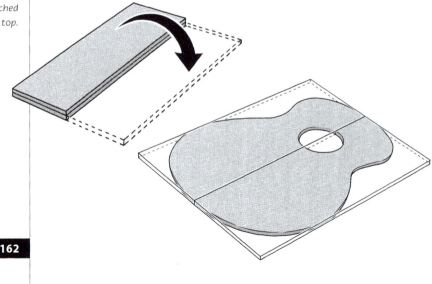

162

The back

The back usually consists of two or three parts. A major difference with the top is that the seams are often finished with a thin strip of wood.

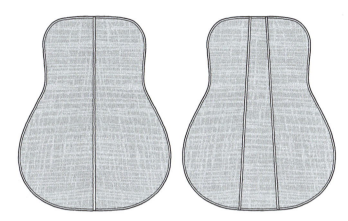

Bookmatched backs, in two or three parts.

The sides

A mold is used to shape the two pieces that make up the sides or rims of the guitar. Alternatively, they may be soaked and then bent, using heat. Thin linings, either with or without saw-cuts, provide sturdiness where the sides meet the top and the back. The edges of the body, and sometimes those of the head and the neck as well, are usually finished with wooden or plastic bindings.

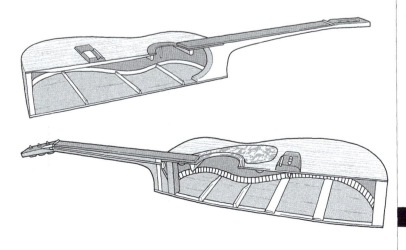

The inside of a classical guitar...

... and the inside of a steel-string guitar.

163

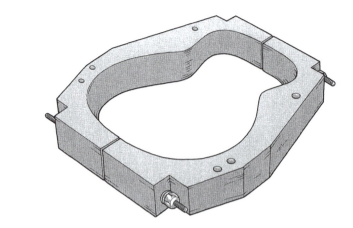

Neck, head, and fingerboard

The neck, heel, and head often look like one solid piece of wood, but they're not. Necks are often made of mahogany; this wood is tough and easy to work with, and it doesn't warp easily. The fingerboard is a separate piece of wood that is glued to the neck.

Dovetail joint

On most steel-string guitars the neck is attached with a so-called dovetail joint, and a similar construction is used for the necks of classical guitars. Glue keeps everything in place. Some steel-string guitars have a bolt-on neck instead.

A dovetail joint on a steel-string guitar.

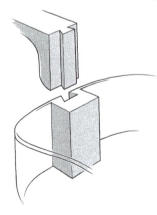

Varnishing and finishing

To finish the guitar, a number of thin coats of varnish, up to ten or more, are applied, each one being polished separately. After the hardware has been mounted, the last steps are the fitting of the strings and a final check.

164

15

Brands

Even if you'd severely limit yourself, a brief description of each and every guitar brand would easily fill up an entire Tipbook — or two. The following chapter introduces some of the main brands, with an indication of product and price ranges.

There are many more guitar brands than there are guitar factories. Many manufacturers make guitars under various brand names. If your order is big enough, you can have your own brand of guitars made pretty much anywhere on the planet. As a result, you may find identical — or almost identical —guitars under different brand names, and they don't always have the same price tag. Most of these 'stencil' instruments are made in Asia.

Current information

The product line of any guitar brand may suddenly be expanded or discontinued, brand names can disappear or be changed, and distribution may stop or commence, so the following is merely an indication of the brands you may come across, and it's by no means intended to be complete.

Please refer to the specialized magazines and websites (see pages 180–182) for up-to-date information on guitar brands and makers.

Nylon and steel

Some brands have both classical and steel-string guitars, as well as electric guitars and bass guitars. Some examples are **Aria** (Japan, 1956), **Hohner** (Germany, 1857), and **Samick** (Korea, 1958). Samick is the trade name of one of the world's biggest guitar manufacturers, supplying instruments for many brands. Other manufacturers make acoustic guitars in pretty much all price ranges, such as the Japanese companies **Takamine**, with its sub-brand **Jasmine**, and **Yamaha**, one of the biggest companies in the music industry, which also makes countless other types of instruments and products.

CLASSICAL GUITARS

Most classical guitars still come from Spain, especially from around its capital Madrid, in the middle of the country, and Valencia, a city on the east coast. Many Spanish brands are not available in the US.

Spanish brands

Some Spanish manufacturers concentrate on the low price range only, others make instruments in various price ranges. When shopping for a Spanish guitar, you can come across dozens of brand names, many actually representing the name of the maker. Some examples of well-known Spanish guitar brands, available in various price-ranges, are **Admira**, **Alhambra**, **Amalio Burguet**, **Cordoba**, **Esteve**, **Manuel Rodriguez**, and **Prudencio Saez**. In Spain, guitars are made in small workshops as well as in large factories where traditional craftsmanship and ultra-modern machinery go hand in hand. Some Spanish companies make other guitars as well, including acoustic-electric and steel-string models.

Concert and student guitars

Professional players easily pay two, three, or five thousand dollars — or even more — for a concert guitar. Most of these instruments are made by luthiers who are known only among very limited audiences. Other 'expensive' luthiers grew bigger, employing several makers, and sometimes even offering student models that are made elsewhere. A few examples? José Ramirez IV is a direct descendant of the **José Ramirez** who made his first guitars in 1882. The last hundred-odd years, members of the Ramirez family taught their trade to countless luthiers in the Madrid area. Some other names are **Contreras**, **Conde Hermanos**, and **Bernabe**, the latter having student models made under the name **Antonio Lopez**.

Japan

Contrary to what you may expect, Japan houses quite a few well-known makers of top-of-the-line 'Spanish' guitars. One example is **Asturias**, with a catalog that includes seven-, ten-, and eleven-string guitars, and a sub-brand (**Kodaira**) representing more affordable models. Concert guitars of more than two thousand dollars are made by Kohno. One of the oldest Japanese makers, **Alvarez-Yairi**, makes both classical and steel-string instruments.

Other countries

Of course, classical guitars are being made in many other countries too, often in one-man workshops.

STEEL-STRING GUITARS

The steel-string acoustic guitar is an American invention, and the traditional steel-string guitar brands, like **Martin** and **Gibson**, are still manufactured there. Most of the lower-priced instruments are made in Asian countries, however, and often marketed under American brand names.

Low, middle, and up
Some brands which can be found both in the lower and the middle price range, sometimes going up to a thousand dollars or more: **Blueridge**, **Cort**, **Crafter**, **Grant**, **Landola**, **Schecter**, **Epiphone**, **Ibanez**, and **Washburn**. The latter three brands are mainly known for their electric guitars. **Dean** is one of the other companies supplying both acoustic and electric guitars, as well as other fretted instruments. The American **Ovation** company fully concentrates on roundback guitars, with its sub-brand **Applause** for the lower price ranges. **Taylor** is a US maker providing a wide variety of guitars, both in the middle and high-end price ranges.

More US brands
Some other US guitar brands, in a variety of price ranges, are **Doolin**, **Froggy Bottom**, **Grimes**, **H.G. Leach**, **Huss & Dalton**, **Klein**, **McPherson**, **Tippin**, and **Wechter**.

Complicated
Alvarez is probably the best brand to show how complicated the guitar industry really is: its Spanish-sounding name, owned by an American company, adorns Korean-made steel-string guitars that were designed by the Japanese luthier Yairi.

Fender and Gibson
The world's most well-known manufacturers of electric guitars, **Fender** and **Gibson**, also market acoustic guitars. Fender and its sub-brand **Squier** concentrate on the lower price ranges, while Gibson makes higher-priced acoustics only.

168

Martin

The **Martin** company, founded in 1833, has been very significant in the development of the steel-string guitar. The current president, C. F. Martin IV, is a namesake and direct descendant of the founder. **Sigma** is their lower-priced range of guitars.

Canada

Canada houses quite a few guitar companies. **Larrivee, Morgan**, and **Thompson** (the latter two former employees of the first) concentrate on the higher mid-range and above. **Garrison**, a recent addition, features a one-piece bracing system. **Godin** has become especially famous for its semi-solid guitars. **Art & Lutherie, Seagull, Simon & Patrick**, and **Norman**, are four steel-string guitar brands coming from the same (Godin) company.

High-end brands

Apart from countless little-known one-man workshops, where you can have a guitar completely custom-made by hand, there's a number of small brands that concentrate on the high-end market — the Irish companies **Larkin** and **Lowden**, for example, or **Lakewood** and **Stevens** from Germany. In America you have, among many others, **Everett, Guild, Tacoma**, and **Breedlove**, the latter founded by former Taylor employees. **RainSong**, from Hawaii, uses graphite instead of wood. A few brands where even the least expensive models cost more, to end this section, are **Baden, Olson, Santa Cruz, Pantheon** and **Dana Bourgeois, Goodall**, and **Collings**.

Glossary

This glossary briefly explains all the guitar jargon used in this Tipbook, and also contains some terms that haven't been mentioned, but which you may come across in other books, magazines, or online. Most terms are explained in more detail as they are introduced in this book. Please consult the index on pages 228–229.

10:1, 12:1, 14:1
A set of 10:1 tuning machines offers faster, but less precise tuning than a set of 12:1 or 14:1 tuners.

Abalone
Mother-of-pearl; product of a shellfish.

Acoustic guitars
In the old days all guitars were acoustic, and they were just called guitars. It was not until electric guitars came along that traditional guitars had to be specified as being 'acoustic.'
Acoustic instruments can be used without an amplifier — and if you need more volume, you can get yourself a so-called acoustic amp.

Acoustic-electric guitar
Acoustic guitar with a pickup and a preamp that can be hooked up directly to an amplifier. Also known as A/E, or as electro-acoustic guitar.

Action
1. The distance between the strings and the fingerboard, also referred to as string height.
2. The 'feel' or ease of playing of a guitar. A guitar with a great action plays really well and easily.

Amplifier
Acoustic amplifiers are specifically designed for acoustic instruments.

Arch-top guitar
A guitar with an arched top and (usually) *f*-shaped soundholes. See also: *Flattop*.

Auditorium, Grand Auditorium
Mid-size steel-string guitars; similar models are known as 000 and 0000, respectively.

Back
The back of the body.

Bass guitar, acoustic
Most acoustic bass guitars have four strings, sounding an octave lower than the four lowest guitar strings.

Bass strings
The lower sounding (wound) strings of a guitar. See also: *Wound strings*.

Binding
Protective and ornamental strips that run around the body and sometimes around the neck and the head as well.

Body
The body of an acoustic guitar acts as a soundbox, acoustically amplifying the vibrations of the strings. Most electric guitars have solid bodies (101–102).

Bookmatched
A bookmatched top consists of two parts that are each other's mirror image.

Bottleneck
Used to play slide guitar.

Bracing
A set of braces underneath the top, which influence the sound and reinforce the wood. Most classical guitars have fan-bracing, while

X-bracing is still very popular on steel-string guitars. Some of the alternatives are horizontal, A- and V-bracings.

Bridge
The strings are attached to the body at the bridge, and run over the saddle or bridge saddle. See also: *Bridge saddle* and *Nut*.

Bridge pins
The pins that secure the strings of a steel-string guitar to the bridge.

Bridge saddle
Thin strip, usually plastic, that supports the strings, just before the point where they're attached to the bridge. Many steel-string guitars have a *compensated saddle*, which is slightly adjusted to enable optimal intonation. See: *Intonation*.

Camber
See: *Radius*.

Capo
By mounting a capo (from the Italian 'capo d'astro') on the neck of a guitar, you can raise the overall pitch in half steps.

Classical guitar
Acoustic guitar with nylon strings. Also referred to as Spanish guitar or nylon-string guitar.

Concert, Grand Concert
Smaller-sized steel-string guitars.

Concert guitar
Expensive classical guitar for professional performances. However, the same name is used for the low-budget models of low-budget brands too. Conversely, some well-known luthiers make 'student guitars' with thousand-dollar price-tags…

Custom
Many luthiers will make guitars exactly according to the customer's specifications. Some expensive brands offer custom options, such as a choice between various necks or tops.

Cutaway
A cutaway allows for easier access to the highest frets.

Dobro
See: *Resonator guitar*.

Dreadnought
Big-size steel-string guitar.

Ebony
Hard type of wood, often used for fingerboards.

Electro-acoustic guitar
See: *Acoustic-electric guitar*.

Element
See: *Pickup*.

Fan-bracing
See: *Bracing*.

Fingerpicking
Steel-string guitar playing style; the thumb takes care of the bass part, the other fingers play the melody.

173

Flageolet
See: *Harmonic.*

Flamenco guitar
Very similar to a classical guitar, but often a bit smaller, with a thin top, one or two pickguards (*golpeador*), and a rather low action.

Flattop
Steel-string guitar with a flat top, as opposed to an arched top. Classical guitars have flat tops too, but there's no need to refer to them as such; there are no classical arch-top guitars. See also: *Arch-top guitar.*

Folk guitar
See: *Steel-string guitar.*

Fourteen-fret neck
A neck that joins the body at the fourteenth fret. Most steel-string guitars have fourteen-fret necks. See also: *Twelve-fret neck.*

Fretboard
See: *Fingerboard.*

Frets
The metal strips on the fingerboard or fretboard.

Golpeador
Spanish for pickguard. See also: *Flamenco guitar.*

Grand Auditorium, Grand Concert
Steel-string guitar sizes.

Harmonic
The tone you hear when striking a string that's not pressed down at

a fret, but lightly touched exactly halfway (above the twelfth fret), or at a third, a quarter (etcetera) of the string's length. Also known as *overtone* or *flageolet.*

Head, headstock
The end of the neck. Classical guitars have slotted heads; most steel-string guitars have a solid head. Another name: *peghead.*

Heel
The thick part where the neck joins the body.

Hygrometer
Device that indicates the degree of air humidity.

Inlay
The markers, the decoration around the soundhole, and also the bindings are often inlaid pieces of wood or other materials. See also: *Abalone.*

Jumbo
The largest type of steel-string guitar.

Laminated
A laminated top, back, or side consists of a number of thin plies of wood. See also: *Solid.*

Lower bout
The lower wide part of the body.

Luthier
Guitar maker (literally: lute maker).

Machine head
One of the many names for tuner or tuning machine.

Markers
Dots, blocks or other inlaid figures that tell you which fret you are at.

Melody strings
See: *Plain strings*.

Nails

Neck
Joins the body and the head.

Notch filter
An adjustable filter that cancels out feedback Found on guitars, amps, and effects. See also: *Feedback*.

Nut
Small part, often plastic, that separates the head and the neck, keeping the strings at the right distance from each other.

Overtone
See: *Harmonic*.

Open tuning
Alternative guitar tuning.

Peg, peghead
See: *Tuner* and *Head*.

Pick
Usually a triangular piece of plastic, in different weights. Playing with a pick gives a more penetrating sound than playing with your fingers. Another name: *plectrum*.

Pickguard
Thin plastic plate that protects the body against scratching picks and nails.

Pickup
A pickup or transducer converts the vibrations of the strings into electrical signals. Acoustic/ electric guitars usually come with piezo-electric pickups that are located under the guitar's bridge saddle. This type of pickup responds to both steel and nylon strings, unlike magnetic pickups. See also: *Acoustic/ electric guitar*.

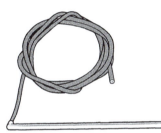

Piezo pickup.

Plectrum
See: *Pick*.

Plain strings
The thin, unwound strings, also called *melody strings* or *trebles*.

Posts
The (string) posts that actually wind the strings.

Preamp, preamplifier
Amplifies the weak signal of a built-in pickup before sending it to the main amp or power amplifier. Most acoustic/ electric guitars have built-in preamps.

Quarter-sawn
When you saw a tree into quarterings, you get stronger wood that allows for the production of

175

thin, yet strong tops. Provides less and therefore more expensive wood than *slab-cutting* trees.

Quarter-sawn wood is stronger that slab-cut wood.

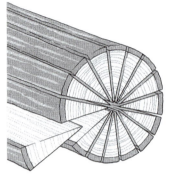

Radius

The curvature of the fingerboard. On steel-string guitars, the fingerboard is a bit rounded; it's higher underneath the middle strings. The degree of this radius or camber is expressed in inches. The higher the number, the flatter the fingerboard.

Resonator guitar

Guitar with amplifying, metal resonators in the top. Also known as *Dobro*, a trade name.

Rosette

The decoration of the soundhole.

Roundback

Guitar with a round back; usually an acoustic-electric instrument.

Saddle

See: *Bridge saddle*.

Scale

The vibrating length of the strings,

measured from the nut to the saddle.

Semi-acoustic guitar

A name often used for arch- top guitars with built-in pickups.

Semi-solid guitar

A guitar with an 'almost but not entirely' solid body.

Sides

Between the top and the back are the sides. They are always made up of two parts, each one running from the heel to the tail of the body.

Slotted bridge

Classical guitars and some (mainly roundback) steel-string guitars have slotted bridges with the strings running through them. See also: *Roundback*.

Slotted head

See: *Head*.

Solid

A solid top, made out of a split, single piece of wood, enhances the sound of a guitar. Some guitars also have solid backs and sides. See also: *Laminated*.

Soundboard

Another word for top. See also: *Top*.

Soundbox

See: *Body*.

Spanish guitar

Another name for classical guitar. Just to make it more confusing, a flamenco guitar is a Spanish guitar too, but it's a different instrument. And there are lots of other countries where 'Spanish' guitars are made... See also: *Classical guitar.*

Steel-string guitar
Generic name to indicate a guitar with steel-strings and a flat top. Also called western guitar, folk guitar, or flat-top guitar.

String posts
See: *Posts.*

String winder
Tool to speed up loosening or tightening strings. Some models help in removing bridge pins too.

Student guitar
See: *Concert guitar.*

Top
The top of the body; also known as soundboard.

Transducer
See: *Pickup.*

Treble strings, trebles
See: *Plain strings.*

Triple-0
Mid-size steel-string guitar, comparable to an Auditorium. See: *Auditorium, Grand Auditorium.*

Truss rod
Usually a metal, adjustable rod that reinforces (trusses) the neck of a steel-string guitar.

Tuner, tuning machine
Each string has its own tuning machine. Classical guitars have open tuners, steel-strings usually have sealed ones.
Some other names are *machine head*, *tuning head*, *tuning key*, and *tuning gear*. The wooden tuners on flamenco guitars are called *pegs*, and this word is used for the tuners of other guitars too.

Twelve-fret neck
A twelve-fret neck has more than twelve frets, but the twelfth fret is the one where the neck joins the body, as on classical guitars. See also: *Fourteen-fret neck.*

Upper bout
Upper, broader part of the body.

Varnish
The type and the quality of the varnish may influence the sound, the appearance, and the way a guitar should be cleaned.

Waist
The narrow part of the body.

Western guitar
Another name for steel-string guitars. See: *Steel-string guitar.*

Wound strings
Strings that are wound with thin metal wire.

X-bracing
See: *Bracing.*

177

Want to Know More?

Tipbooks supply you with basic information on the instrument of your choice, and everything that comes with it. Of course there's a lot more to be found on all of the subjects you came across on these pages. This section offers a selection of magazines, books, helpful websites, and more.

MAGAZINES

Some of these magazines concentrate on acoustic guitars, others focus on electric instruments but include acoustics as well, still others concentrate on a certain style of guitar playing.

* *Acoustic Guitar*, www.acguitar.com

* *Fingerstyle Guitar*, www.fingerstyleguitar.com

* *Flatpicking Guitar*, www.flatpick.com

* *Guitar Digest*, www.guitardigest.com

* *Guitar One*, www.guitarworld.com/guitarone

* *Guitar Player*, www.guitarplayer.com

* *Guitar Review*, www.guitarreview.com

* *Guitar Techniques* (UK), www.futurenet.com

* *Guitar World*, www.guitarworld.com

* *Vintage Guitar*, www.vintageguitar.com

BOOKS

There are countless books on guitars, including publications dedicated to one guitar brand only. The list below contains a variety of books, some concentrating on the history of the instrument, others more technically oriented, some also including electric guitars and basses, others dedicated to acoustic instruments only. Please note that this list is not intended to be complete, and that some books may have been reprinted by the time you read this.

* *The Ultimate Guitar Book*, Tony Bacon and Paul Day (Knopf, 1997; 192 pages; ISBN 978-0375700903).

* *The Guitar Handbook*, Ralph Denyer (Knopf, 1992; 256 pages; ISBN 978-0679742753).

* *The Complete Guitarist* (Richard Chapman, DK Adult, England, 2003; 208 pages; ISBN 978-0789497017).

* *The Acoustic Guitar Guide*, Larry Sandberg (Chicago Review Press, 2000; 304 pages; ISBN 978-1556524189).

- *Acoustic Guitar Owner's Manual – The Complete Guide* (String Letter, Hal Leonard, 2000; 96 pages; ISBN 978-1890490218).

- *American Guitars – An Illustrated History,* Tom Wheeler (Harper Resource, 1992; 384 pages; ISBN 978-0062731548).

- *Custom Guitars – A Complete Guide to Contemporary Handcrafted Guitars* (String Letter, 2000; 151 pages; ISBN 978-1890490294).

- *Gruhn's Guide to Vintage Guitars – An Identification Guide for American Fretted Instruments,* George Gruhn, Walter Carter (Backbeat Books, 1999; 582 pages; ISBN 978-0879304225).

- *Acoustic Guitars and Other Fretted Instruments – A Photographic History,* George Gruhn, Walter Carter (Backbeat Books, 1997; 320 pages; ISBN 978-0879304935).

- *Blue Book of Acoustic Guitars,* by Zachary R. Fjestad (Blue/Black, 11th edition, 2007; 750 pages; ISBN 978-1886768741; check for updated editions).

- *The Acoustic Guitar,* Nick Freeth and Charles Alexander (Courage Books, USA/UK, 1999; 159 pages; ISBN 978-0762404193).

- *The Guitar Player Repair Guide,* Dan Erlewine (Backbeat Books, 2007. DVD included; 322 pages; ISBN 978-0879309213).

- *2008 Official Vintage Guitar Magazine Price Guide,* Alan Greenwood and Gil Hembree (Vintage Guitar Books, 2007; 520 pages; ISBN 978-1884883194; check for updated editions).

- *Guitarmaking: Tradition and Technology: A Complete Reference for the Design & Construction of the Steel-String Folk Guitar & the Classical Guitar* (Chronicle Books, 1998; 392 pages; ISBN 978-0811806404).

INTERNET

You can find tons of guitar information online. Below are some links to informative websites that also offer links to other sites (ranging from guitar makers and teachers to online lessons) and other services.

- www.acoustic-guitars.net
- www.guitar.com
- www.guitarist.com
- www.guitarnotes.com
- www.guitarnotes.com/rmmga
- www.guitarsite.com
- www.guitartips.addr.com
- www.harmony-central.com/acoustic-guitar
- www.museweb.com/ag
- www.wholenote.com
- www.worldguitarist.com

Also check out the websites of magazines listed above!

Looking for a teacher?

If you want to find a teacher online, try searching for "guitar teacher" and the name of the area or city where you live, or visit one of the following special interest websites:

- PrivateLessons.com: www.privatelessons.com
- MusicStaff.com: www.musicstaff.com
- The Music Teachers List: www.teachlist.com

Guild of American Luthiers

If you would like to learn to make guitars yourself, you could contact the Guild of American Luthiers (www.luth.org). Their website lists lutherie schools and information on online instruction, and more.

Tipcode List

The Tipcodes in this book offer easy access to short videos, sound files, and other additional information at www.tipbook.com. For your convenience, the Tipcodes in this Tipbook have been listed below.

Tipbook Chord Diagrams

This chapter features chord diagrams of a large variety of popular guitar chords. Each chord is shown in both beginner and advanced positions. An introduction on how chords are constructed is also included!

As explained in Chapter 3, a chord diagram shows you where to fret the strings to play a specific chord. Basic chord diagrams allow you to easily learn to play hundreds, if not thousands of popular songs.

Diagrams

The chord diagrams on pages 190–220 show you a lot more than where to put your fingers.

An '**X**' indicates strings that should not sound along. An '**X**' in parentheses: **(X)** tells you that you can choose to make that string sound along or not.

This arrow points down at the lowest sounding root note of the chord.

Hollow dots indicate the open strings. A hollow dot in parentheses: **(O)** tells you that you can choose to make that open string sound along or not.

This black line is a barre, fretting multiple strings with your index finger (1)

Solid dots tell you where to fret the strings. The number indicates the appropriate finger.

These are the sounding notes of each chord.

These are the intervals of the chord (see page 188).

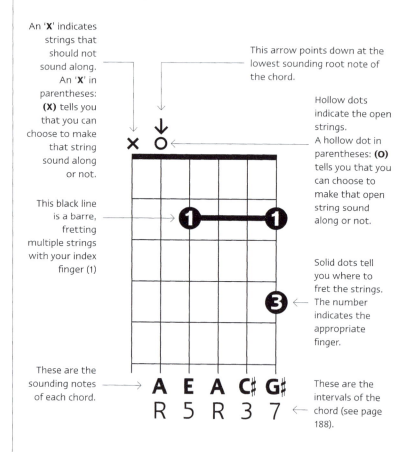

Tabs

Chords can be written down using tabs too, the figures indicating where to fret the strings. The first figure or symbol refers to the low E-string, the second to the A-string, and so on. A '0' indicates an open string; an 'X' indicates strings that should not be played. This way, the upper D7 chord on page 200 looks as follows: X-X-0-2-1-2.

Vertical tabs

Some prefer a vertical tab notation, either from low E to high E or the other way around. Here's a brief chord progression.

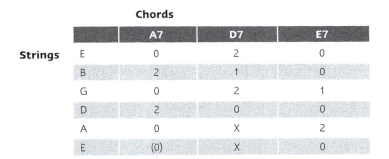

		Chords		
		A7	**D7**	**E7**
Strings	E	0	2	0
	B	2	1	0
	G	0	2	1
	D	2	0	0
	A	0	X	2
	E	(0)	X	0

Chord construction

There are many different types of chords: major chords, minor chords, diminished chords, and so on. Every specific type of chord is constructed the same way, using a root note and two or more other notes. How this works is explained on pages 188–189.

Table

The table on pages 186–187 shows the names, the chord symbols, and the intervals of a variety of chord types, including an example (in C) for each type of chord. The chords in the lower section of this table have not been included in the chord diagrams in this book.

Inversions

Each chord can be played in various ways. These so-called *inversions* can make a chord sound higher or lower — depending on how high it is on the neck — but they also make chords sound differently, with another timbre or nature. You can use this musically, of course, by choosing your chords and inversions so that your chord progressions get a nice flow, for example. Other than that, knowing the various ways to play each chord can make

Chord symbol	Alternative symbols	Chord tones
C	–	C, E, G
Cmaj^7	CM^7, C$^\Delta$	C, E, G, B
C7	Cdom^7	C, E, G, B♭
C6	Cmaj^6	C, E, G, A
C9	–	C, E, G, B♭, D
Cm	C–, Cmi, Cmin	C, E♭, G
Cm^7	C–^{7}, Cmi^7, Cmin^7	C, E♭, G, B♭
Cm^9	C–^{9}, Cmi^9, Cmin^9	C, E♭, G, B♭, D
Csus4	Csus	C, F, G
Cadd9	–	C, E, G, D
C7sus4	–	C, F, G, B♭
Csus2	–	C, D, G
Caug	C+, C^{+5}, C$^{\sharp5}$	C, E, G♯
Cdim	C$^\circ$, C$^{\circ7}$, C^{-7}, Cdim^7	C, E♭, G♭, A
C$^{♭5}$	–	C, E, G♭
C7$^{♭9}$	C7^{-9}	C, E, G, B♭, D♭
Cm^6	C–^{6}, Cmin^6	C, E♭, G, A
Cm$^{7(♭5)}$	C$^\varnothing$, C–$^{7(♭5)}$	C, E♭, G♭, B♭
Cmi^{ma7}	C–$^\Delta$, Cm$^\Delta$, Cm$^{(maj7)}$	C, E♭, G, B

it easier to go from one chord to the next. The chord diagrams presented in this book show both the basic chord and various inversions for each chord.

TIP

Beginner's chords

In some cases, inversions are easier to play than the basic chords shown in the upper rows on pages 190–213. Still, beginners are adviced to initially focus on those 'upper' chords.

Powerchords

Page 214 shows various *powerchords*. These are relatively easy to play, 'powerful' chords consisting of the root note and the fifth of a chord only. You can play them on no more than two strings,

188

Intervals (1=R)	Chord name
1, 3, 5	C major
1, 3, 5, 7	C major seven
1, 3, 5, ♭7	C seven, C dominant seven
1, 3, 5, 6	C six
1, 3, 5, ♭7, 9	C nine
1, ♭3, 5	C minor
1, ♭3, 5, ♭7	C minor seven
1, ♭3, 5, ♭7, 9	C minor nine
1, 4, 5	C suspended (four)
1, 3, 5, 9	C add nine
1, 4, 5, ♭7	C seven sus four
1, 2, 5	C suspended (two)
1, 3, ♯5	C augmented
1, ♭3, ♭5, ♭7 (=6)	C diminished
1, 3, ♭5	C flat five
1, 3, 5, ♭7, ♭9	C seven flat nine
1, ♭3, 5, 6	C minor six
1, ♭3, ♭5, ♭7	C half diminished, C-minor flat five
1, ♭3, 5, 7	C minor/major seven

but most players use three, sounding one or two root notes (an octave apart) and one or two fifths (also an octave apart).

More chords

- Pages 215–219 show a number of movable chords, both with and without barre.

- Numerous songs use no more than three different chords. How this works and which chords such songs often use is explained on page 221.

- Some examples of popular chord progressions in various styles of music can be found on pages 222–225.

- You can find many more chords (and tabs, songs, etc.) online. Some interesting websites are listed on page 225.

CHORD CONSTRUCTION

Chord construction is not really that complex. Each chord has a root note.

- In C major, C minor, C dim or any other C chord, the root note is C.

- In C major, the second note of the chord sounds a major third higher than the root note (E).

- In C major, the third note of the chord sounds a perfect fifth higher than the root note (G).

If you put these steps in a row, C major looks like R (root) – 3 (major third) – 5 (perfect fifth).

Minor chords
In a minor chord, the second step is a minor third rather than a major third. This means that the second note of the chord is lowered by a half step. C minor is C–E♭–G (R–♭3–5).

Diminished, augmented
In a diminished chord, the fifth is also lowered (R–♭3–♭5); an augmented chord has a raised fifth (R–3–♯5). So each type of chord has its own specific construction.

Four
All chords listed so far are made up of three notes. There are also chords that use four or more notes, the extra notes being added to the three notes of the basic chord. These extra notes are often indicated using digits. The table on pages 186–187 includes some examples of these types of chords.

- The digit 7 in a chord symbol tells you to add a minor seventh to the chord. C7 is C–E–G–B♭ (R–3–5–♭7).

- The addition maj7 adds a major seventh to the chord (C–E–G–B or R–3–5–7).

- A 6 tells you to add a major sixth (C–E–G–A or R–3–5–6).

190

- Other additions speak for themselves. A♭5 lowers the fifth a half step (C–E–G♭); a 9 adds a high D (and a B♭) to the C-chord, ♭9 adds a D♭ and ♯9 a D♯, and so on. There are also 11 and 13 chords.

- Some chord inversions can make it necessary or desirable to leave out certain notes of a chord, such as the 5, the 7 or even the root note. If there's no root note in a chord, this can be indicated by the letters NR (no root).

191

A

Legend	
Barre	❶–❶
Fret with 2nd finger	❷
Fretting is optional	❹
Fret with thumb	Ⓣ
Lowest root note	↓
Don't play this string	×
Open string	o
Don't play (optional)	(x)
Open string (optional)	(O)

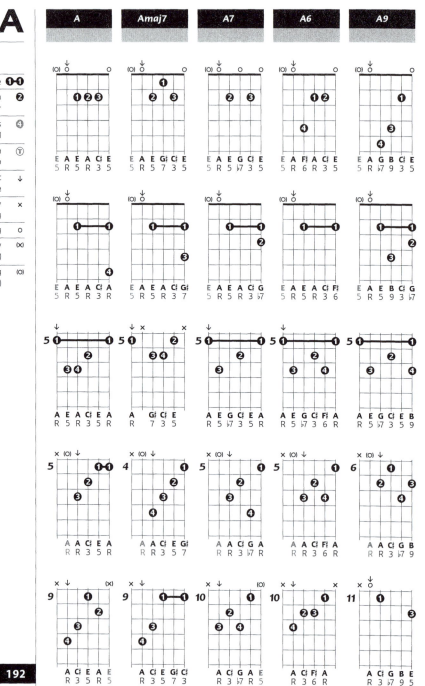

A   Amaj7   A7   A6   A9

A

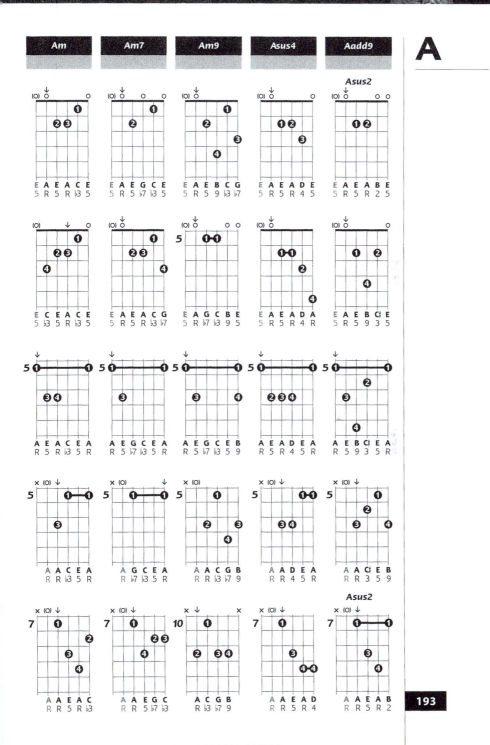

| Am | Am7 | Am9 | Asus4 | Aadd9 |

B♭

Enharmonic: **A♯**

Barre	❶-❶
Fret with 2nd finger	❷
Fretting is optional	❹
Fret with thumb	Ⓣ
Lowest root note	↓
Don't play this string	×
Open string	o
Don't play (optional)	(×)
Open string (optional)	(o)

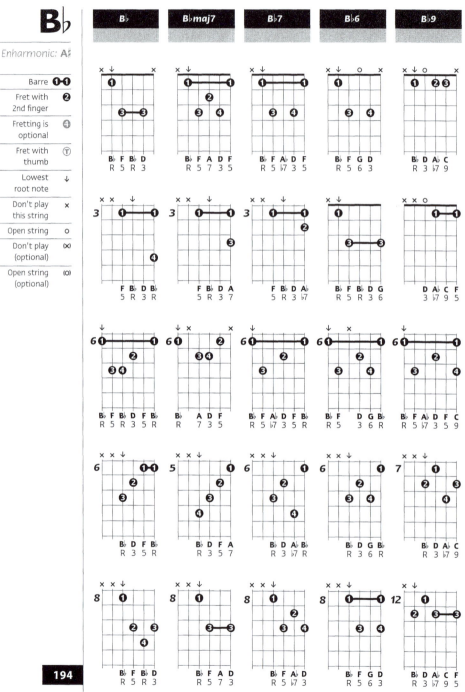

194

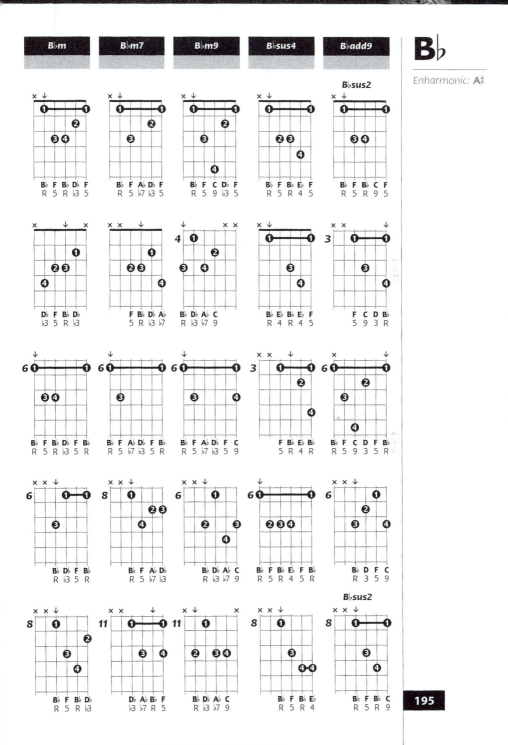

B♭

Enharmonic: **A♯**

B♭m	B♭m7	B♭m9	B♭sus4	B♭add9

B

| B | Bmaj7 | B7 | B6 | B9 |

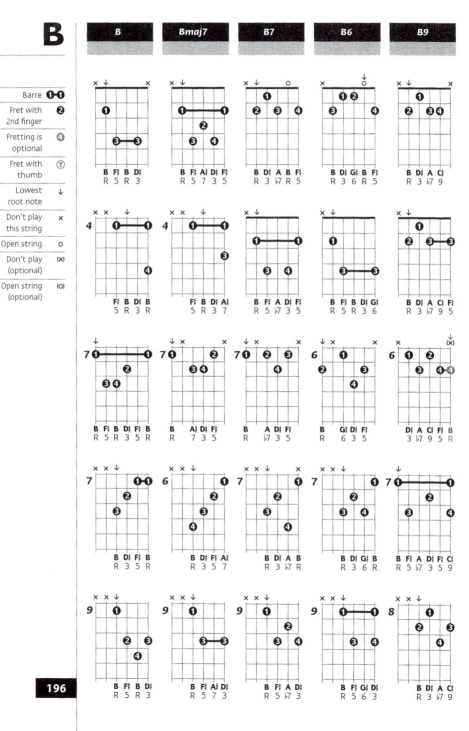

Barre **❶–❶**

Fret with **❷**
2nd finger

Fretting is **❹**
optional

Fret with **Ⓣ**
thumb

Lowest ↓
root note

Don't play ✕
this string

Open string o

Don't play (✕)
(optional)

Open string (O)
(optional)

196

B

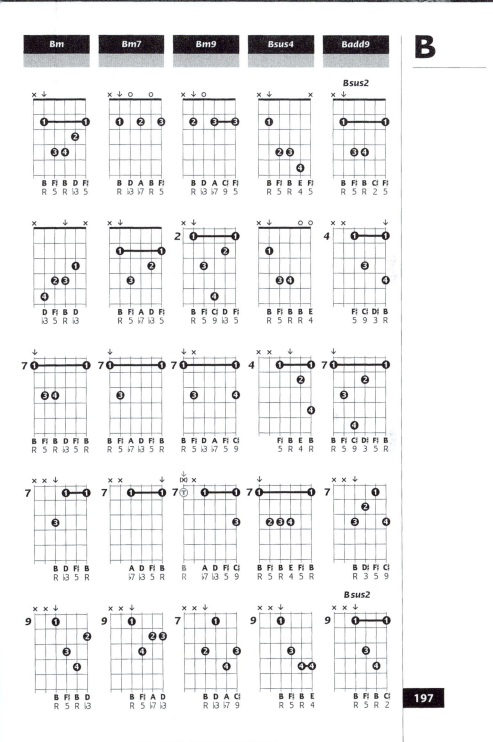

| Bm | Bm7 | Bm9 | Bsus4 | Badd9 |

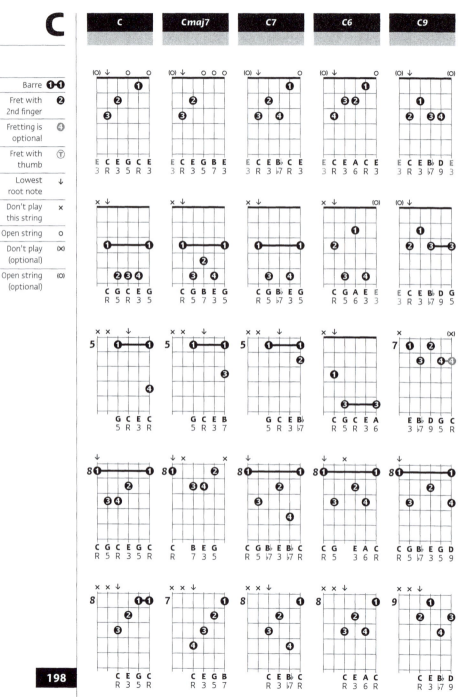

Barre 🐵🐵
Fret with 2nd finger ➋
Fretting is optional ➍
Fret with thumb Ⓣ
Lowest root note ↓
Don't play this string ✕
Open string ○
Don't play (optional) (✕)
Open string (optional) (○)

198

C

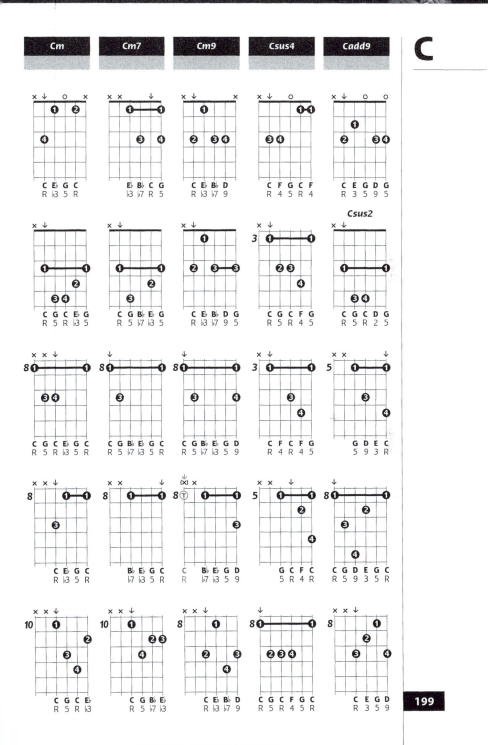

| Cm | Cm7 | Cm9 | Csus4 | Cadd9 |

Csus2

D♭

Enharmonic: **C♯**

Barre	❶–❶
Fret with 2nd finger	❷
Fretting is optional	❹
Fret with thumb	Ⓣ
Lowest root note	↓
Don't play this string	×
Open string	o
Don't play (optional)	(×)
Open string (optional)	(O)

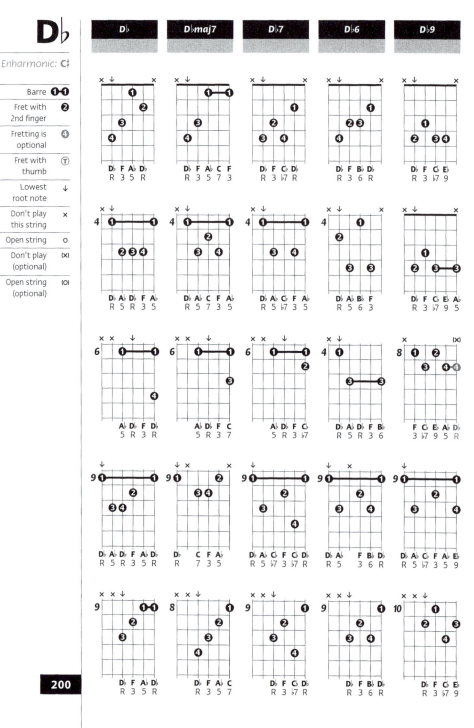

D♭	D♭maj7	D♭7	D♭6	D♭9

Row 1:
- D♭ F A♭ D♭ / R 3 5 R
- D♭ F A♭ C F / R 3 5 7 3
- D♭ F C♭ D♭ / R 3 ♭7 R
- D♭ F B♭ D♭ / R 3 6 R
- D♭ F C♭ E♭ / R 3 ♭7 9

Row 2:
- D♭ A♭ D♭ F A♭ / R 5 R 3 5
- D♭ A♭ C F A♭ / R 5 7 3 5
- D♭ A♭ C♭ F A♭ / R 5 ♭7 3 5
- D♭ A♭ B♭ F / R 5 6 3
- D♭ F C♭ E♭ A♭ / R 3 ♭7 9 5

Row 3:
- A♭ D♭ F D♭ / 5 R 3 R
- A♭ D♭ F C / 5 R 3 7
- A♭ D♭ F C♭ / 5 R 3 ♭7
- D♭ A♭ D♭ F B♭ / R 5 R 3 6
- F C♭ E♭ A♭ D♭ / 3 ♭7 9 5 R

Row 4:
- D♭ A♭ D♭ F A♭ D♭ / R 5 R 3 5 R
- D♭ C F A♭ / R 7 3 5
- D♭ A♭ C♭ F C♭ D♭ / R 5 ♭7 3 ♭7 R
- D♭ A♭ F B♭ D♭ / R 5 3 6 R
- D♭ A♭ C♭ F A♭ E♭ / R 5 ♭7 3 5 9

Row 5:
- D♭ F A♭ D♭ / R 3 5 R
- D♭ F A♭ C / R 3 5 7
- D♭ F C♭ D♭ / R 3 ♭7 R
- D♭ F B♭ D♭ / R 3 6 R
- D♭ F C♭ E♭ / R 3 ♭7 9

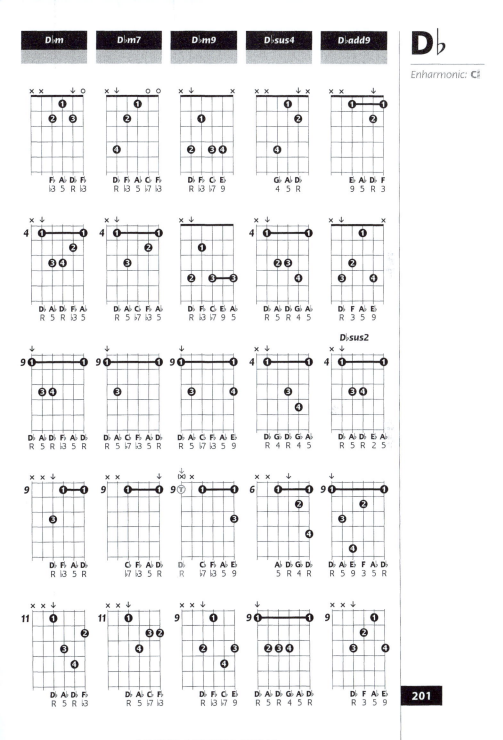

Db | **Dbm7** | **Dbm9** | **Dbsus4** | **Dbadd9**

Db

Enharmonic: C#

Dbsus2

D

Barre ❶–❶

Fret with 2nd finger ❷

Fretting is optional ④

Fret with thumb Ⓣ

Lowest root note ↓

Don't play this string ✗

Open string o

Don't play (optional) (✗)

Open string (optional) (O)

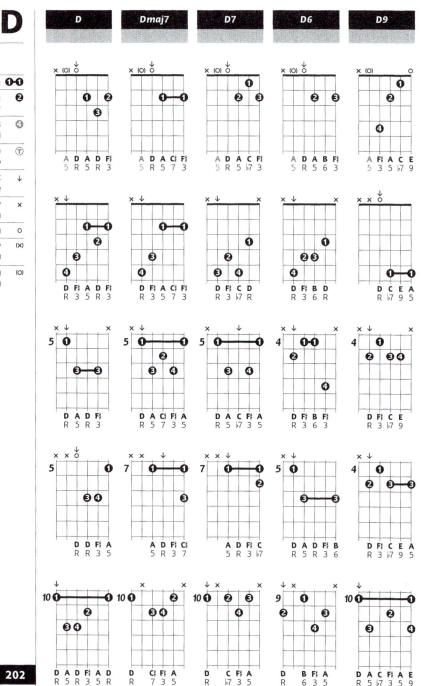

202

D

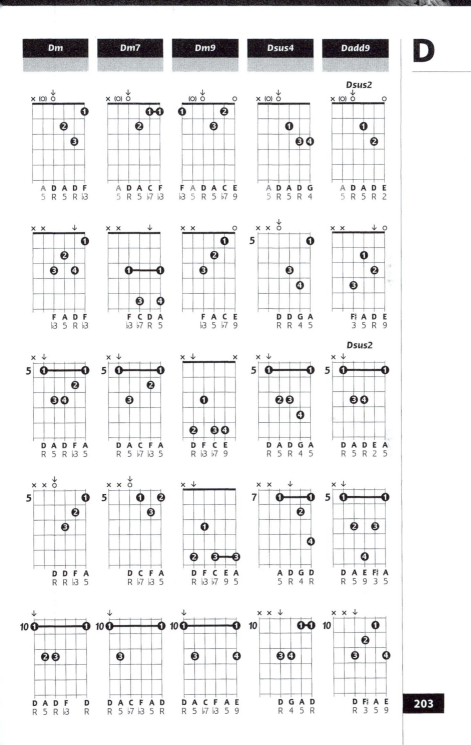

Dm	Dm7	Dm9	Dsus4	Dadd9

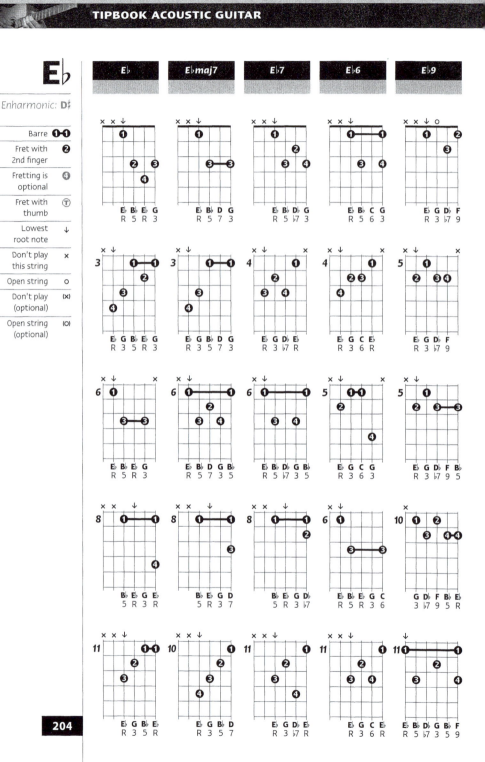

E♭

Enharmonic: **D♯**

Barre	**❶–❶**
Fret with 2nd finger	**❷**
Fretting is optional	**❹**
Fret with thumb	**Ⓣ**
Lowest root note	↓
Don't play this string	×
Open string	o
Don't play (optional)	(×)
Open string (optional)	(O)

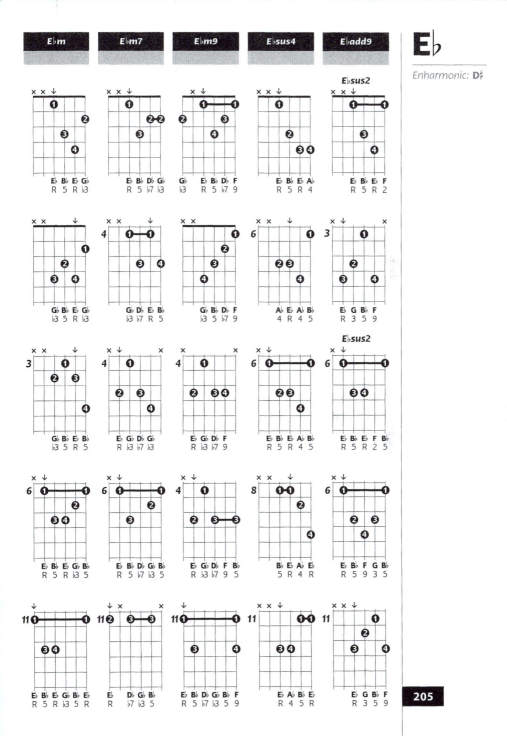

E♭

Enharmonic: **D♯**

E

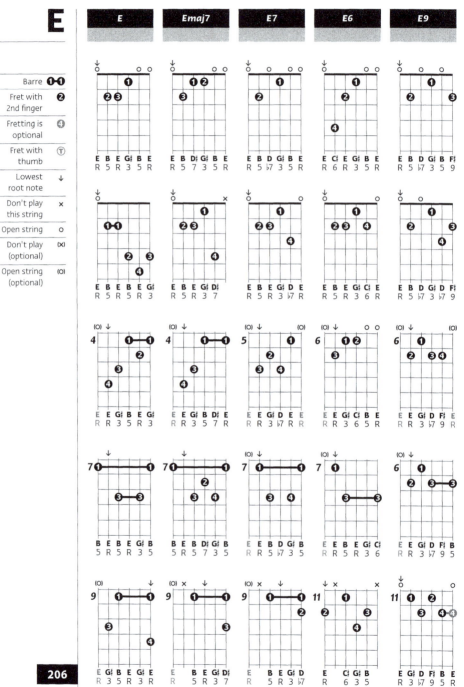

Barre
Fret with 2nd finger
Fretting is optional
Fret with thumb
Lowest root note
Don't play this string
Open string
Don't play (optional)
Open string (optional)

206

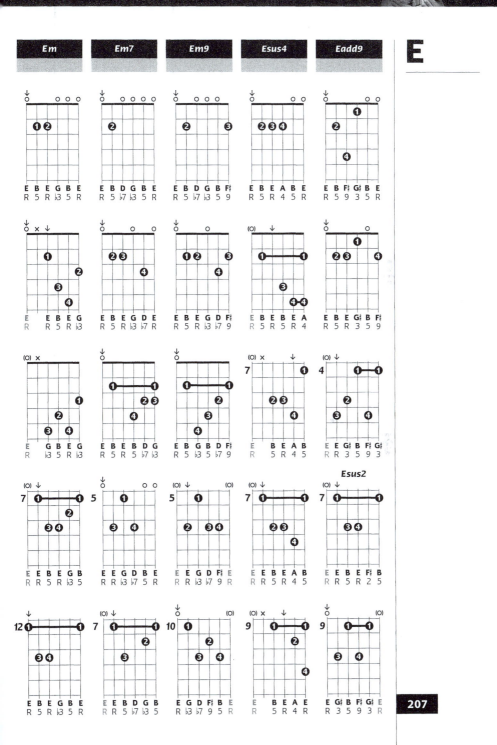

E

207

F

Barre ❶–❶

Fret with 2nd finger ❷

Fretting is optional ❹

Fret with thumb Ⓣ

Lowest root note ↓

Don't play this string ✕

Open string o

Don't play (optional) (✕)

Open string (optional) (O)

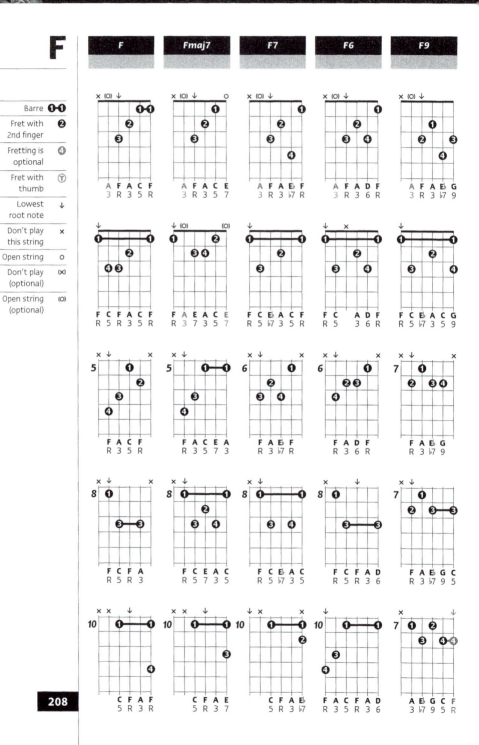

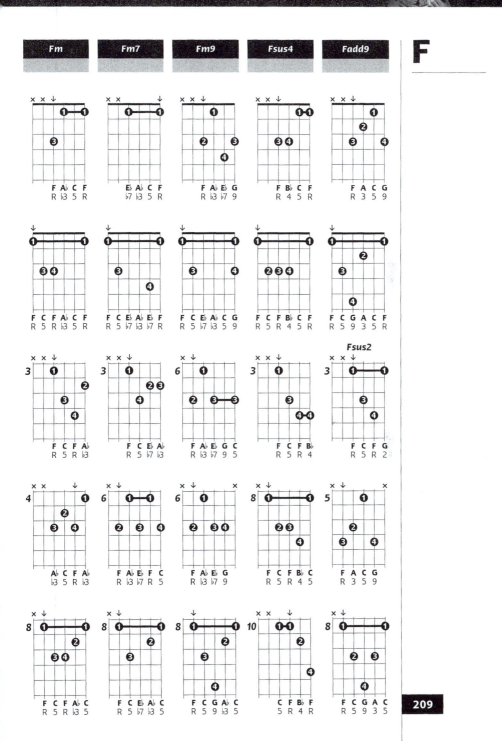

F#

Enharmonic: **G♭**

Barre	❶-❶
Fret with 2nd finger	❷
Fretting is optional	❹
Fret with thumb	Ⓣ
Lowest root note	↓
Don't play this string	×
Open string	o
Don't play (optional)	(×)
Open string (optional)	(o)

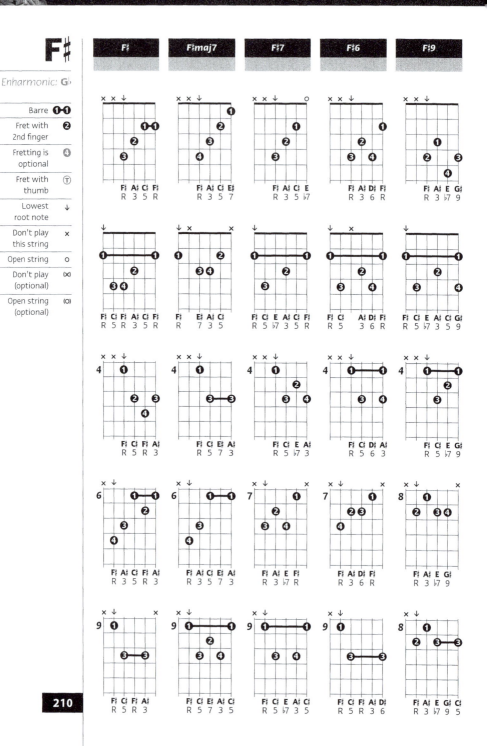

F#	F#maj7	F#7	F#6	F#9
F# A# C# F# R 3 5 R	F# A# C# E# R 3 5 7	F# A# C# E R 3 5 ♭7	F# A# D# F# R 3 6 R	F# A# E G# R 3 ♭7 9
F# C# F# A# C# F# R 5 R 3 5 R	F# E# A# C# R 7 3 5	F# C# E A# C# F# R 5 ♭7 3 5 R	F# C# A# D# F# R 5 3 6 R	F# C# E A# C# G# R 5 ♭7 3 5 9
F# C# F# A# R 5 R 3	F# C# E# A# R 5 7 3	F# C# E A# R 5 ♭7 3	F# C# D# A# R 5 6 3	F# C# E G# R 5 ♭7 9
F# A# C# F# A# R 3 5 R 3	F# A# C# E# A# R 3 5 7 3	F# A# E F# R 3 ♭7 R	F# A# D# F# R 3 6 R	F# A# E G# R 3 ♭7 9
F# C# F# A# R 5 R 3	F# C# E# A# C# R 5 7 3 5	F# C# E A# C# R 5 ♭7 3 5	F# C# F# A# D# R 5 R 3 6	F# A# E G# C# R 3 ♭7 9 5

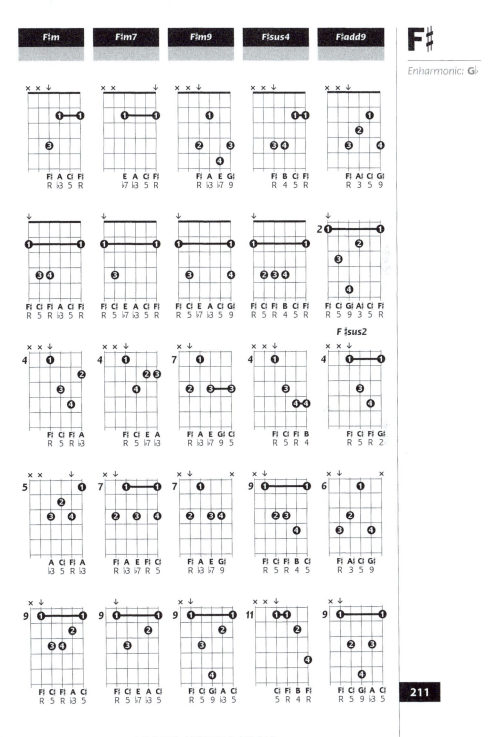

F#

Enharmonic: **G♭**

G

Barre
Fret with 2nd finger
Fretting is optional
Fret with thumb
Lowest root note
Don't play this string
Open string
Don't play (optional)
Open string (optional)

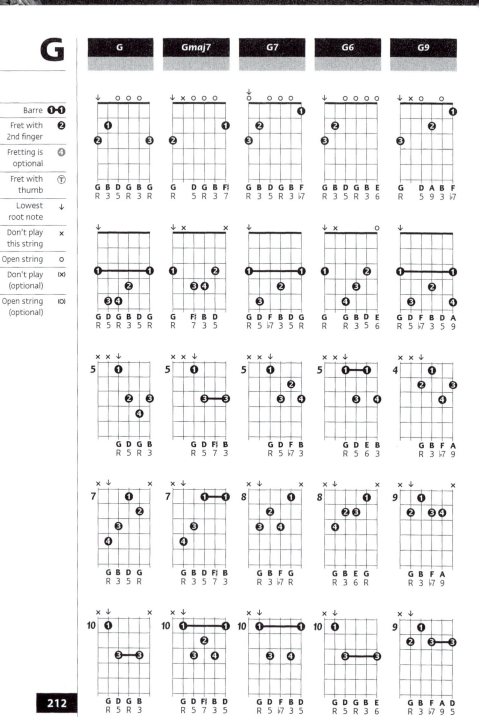

G

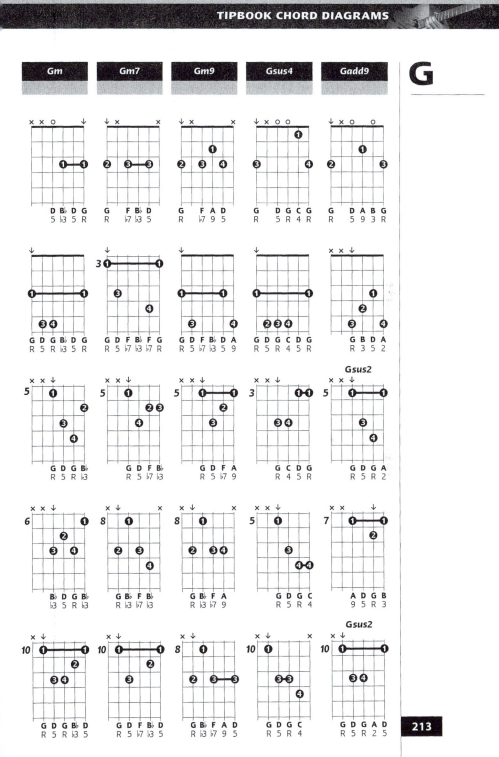

A♭

Enharmonic: **G♯**

Barre	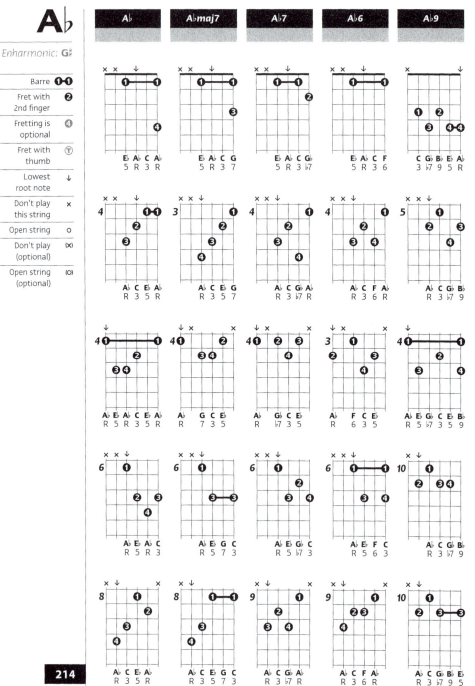
Fret with 2nd finger	❷
Fretting is optional	❹
Fret with thumb	Ⓣ
Lowest root note	↓
Don't play this string	×
Open string	o
Don't play (optional)	(×)
Open string (optional)	(O)

214

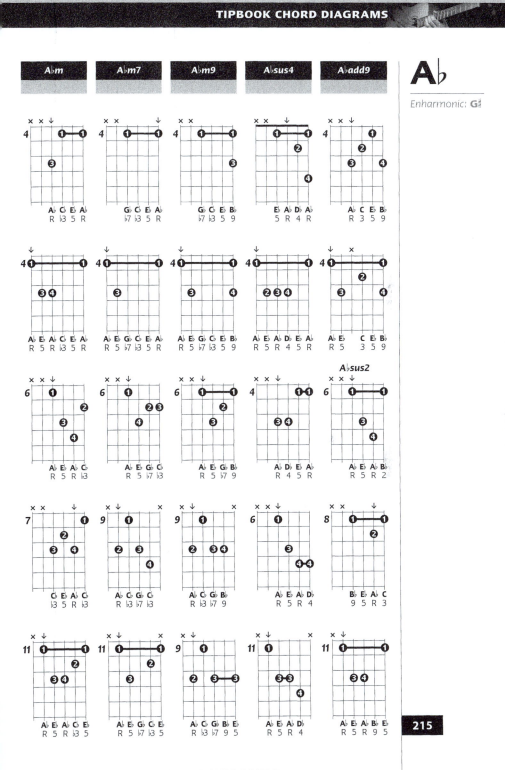

A♭

Enharmonic: G♯

POWERCHORDS

The powerchords (see page 186) on this page are easy to play. They're mainly used in pop and heavy metal.

OPEN POWER CHORDS

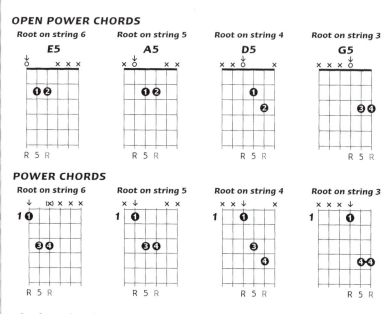

The four chords above are movable power chords in the first position (F5, A♯/B♭5, D♯/E♭5, and G♯/A♭5 respectively). Each time you move them one fret up, they will sound a half step higher. The table below shows the resulting chords in the first six positions.

1 F5	1 A♯5 – B♭5	1 D♯5–E♭5	1 G♯5 – A♭5
2 F♯5 – G♭5	2 B5	2 E5	2 A5
3 G5	3 C5	3 F5	3 A♯5 – B♭5
4 G♯5 – A♭5	4 C♯5 – D♭5	4 F♯5 – G♭5	4 B5
5 A5	5 D5	5 G5	5 C5
6 A♯5 – B♭5	6 D♯5–E♭5	6 G♯5 – A♭5	6 C♯5 – D♭5
etc.	etc.	etc.	etc.

BARRE AND MOVABLE CHORDS

There is a large group of chords that you can simply move along the neck of your instrument. Many of these *movable chords* use a barre, fretting two or more strings with your index finger. These chords are known as *movable barre chords*.

Example
The F major barre chord is a well-known example of a movable barre chord. Move the chord from the first to the second position on your guitar, and you'll hear the same chord a half step higher (F♯). Move it up another fret and you'll hear G major — and so on. The guitar necks and tables on pages 216-217 show you the root note for each position.

The top nut
F major is actually the same chord 'shape' as E major — but in E major, the top nut replaces the barre.

No barre
Other movable chord shapes do not use a barre (pages 218–219). The root note of these chords is indicated by an arrow and/or the letter R below the chord chart.

Open tuning
If a song uses one type of chords only, you can tune your guitar to that chord (open tunings; see page 125). If you do so, you can play the entire song by simply fretting all strings simultaneously (using your index finger or a slide; see page 125) and moving up and down the neck.

Examples
A large number of movable chords has already been included in the chord diagrams on the previous pages. The next four pages show you additional examples of barre and movable chords respectively.

217

Barre Chords

Basic chord

Barre chord

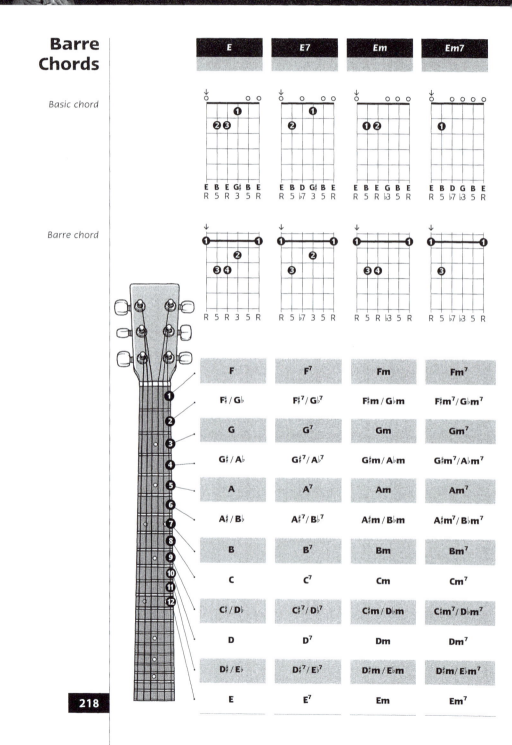

E	E7	Em	Em7

Basic chord:

E B E G# B E	E B D G# B E	E B E G B E	E B D G B E
R 5 R 3 5 R	R 5 b7 3 5 R	R 5 R b3 5 R	R 5 b7 b3 5 R

Barre chord:

R 5 R 3 5 R	R 5 b7 3 5 R	R 5 R b3 5 R	R 5 b7 b3 5 R

F	F7	Fm	Fm7
F#/Gb	F#7/Gb7	F#m/Gbm	F#m7/Gbm7
G	G7	Gm	Gm7
G#/Ab	G#7/Ab7	G#m/Abm	G#m7/Abm7
A	A7	Am	Am7
A#/Bb	A#7/Bb7	A#m/Bbm	A#m7/Bbm7
B	B7	Bm	Bm7
C	C7	Cm	Cm7
C#/Db	C#7/Db7	C#m/Dbm	C#m7/Dbm7
D	D7	Dm	Dm7
D#/Eb	D#7/Eb7	D#m/Ebm	D#m7/Ebm7
E	E7	Em	Em7

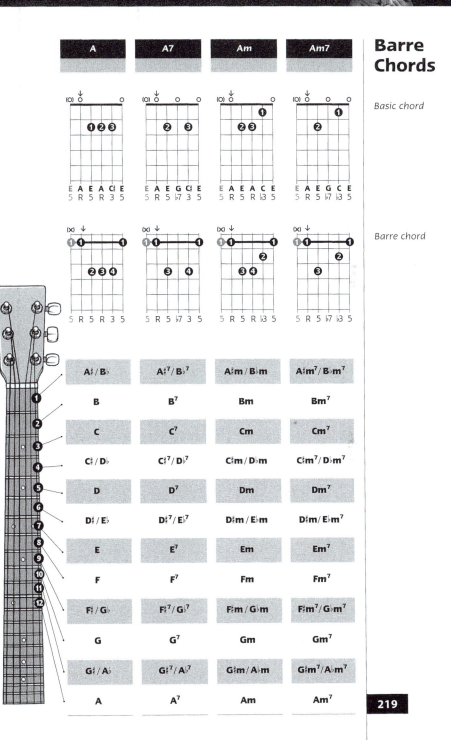

Barre Chords

Basic chord

Barre chord

Movable Chords

Barre	
Fret with 2nd finger	❷
Fretting is optional	❹
Fret with thumb	ⓣ
Lowest root note	↓
Don't play this string	×
Open string	o
Don't play (optional)	(×)
Open string (optional)	(o)

Major Root on string 6	Major Root on string 5	Major Root on string 4	9	Augmented

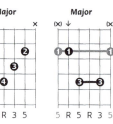

Major — R R 3 5

Major — 5 R 5 R 3 5

Major — 5 R 3 5 R

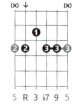 — 5 R 3 ♭7 9 5

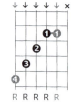 — R R R R R

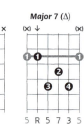

Major 7 (Δ) — R 7 3 5

Major 7 (Δ) — 5 R 5 7 3 5

Major 7 (Δ) — 5 R 3 5 7

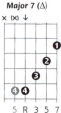 — R 3 ♭7 9 5 R

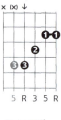 — R R R R

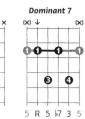

Dominant 7 — R ♭7 3 5

Dominant 7 — 5 R 5 ♭7 3 5

Dominant 7 — 5 R 3 ♭7 R

 — R 5 R 3 ♭7 9

sus 4 — R 5 R 4 5 R

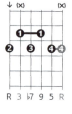

Major 6 — R 6 3 5

Major 6 — R 5 6 3

Major 6 — 5 R 3 6 5

— R 5 ♭7 3 5 9

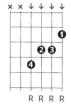 — 5 R 5 R 4 R

Dom 7♯5 — R ♭7 3 ♯5

Dom 7♯5 — R ♯5 ♭7 3

Dom 7♯5 — R ♯5 ♭7 3 ♯5

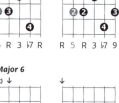 — R 3 ♭7 9 5 R

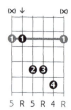 — 5 R 5 R 4

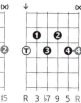

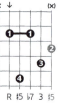

220

Movable Chords

Minor	Minor	Minor	Minor 9	Diminished (O)
Root on string 6	Root on string 5	Root on string 4		

Minor

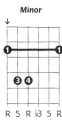 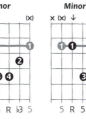 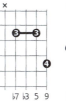 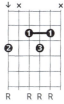

R 5 R ♭3 5 R 5 R 5 R ♭3 5 5 R 5 R ♭3 R ♭7 ♭3 5 9 R R R

Min Maj 7 (Δ)

R 5 7 ♭3 5 5 R 5 7 ♭3 5 5 R 5 7 ♭3 5 R ♭3 ♭7 9 R R R R

Minor 7

R ♭7 ♭3 5 R 5 R 5 ♭7 ♭3 5 5 R 5 ♭7 ♭3 5 R ♭3 ♭7 9 R R R R

Minor 6

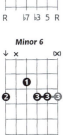 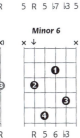 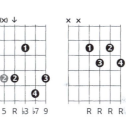 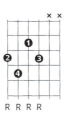

R 6 ♭3 5 R R 5 6 ♭3 5 R 5 6 ♭3 ♭7 ♭3 5 9 R R R

Minor 7♭5 (Ø)

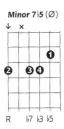 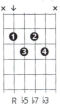 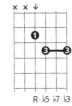 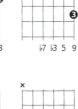

R ♭7 ♭3 ♭5 R ♭5 ♭7 ♭3 R ♭5 ♭7 ♭3 R ♭3 ♭7 9 5

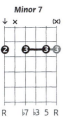

221

CAPO

A capo allows you to play a song any number of half steps higher while using the same chord shapes. This can be handy if, for example, a song is too low for your vocal range, or for the singer you're playing with. Below are four examples of chords that are played with a capo at the third fret.

A capo at the second fret makes chords sound a whole step higher.

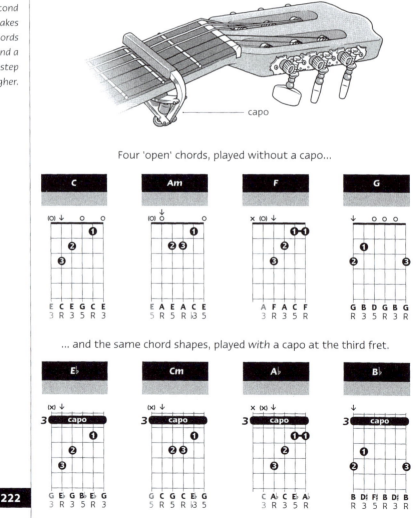

capo

Four 'open' chords, played without a capo...

C	Am	F	G
E C E G C E	E A E A C E	A F A C F	G B D G B G
3 R 3 5 R 3	5 R 5 R ♭3 5	3 R 3 5 R	R 3 5 R 3 R

... and the same chord shapes, played *with* a capo at the third fret.

E♭	Cm	A♭	B♭
G E♭ G B♭ E♭ G	G C G C E♭ G	C A♭ C E♭ A♭	B D♯ F♯ B D♯ B
3 R 3 5 R 3	5 R 5 R ♭3 5	3 R 3 5 R	R 3 5 R 3 R

THREE CHORDS: I, IV, V

Many pop songs use no more than three chords. A very common chord progression uses the chords I, IV and V (one, four, five, in Roman numerals): If the first chord is C (I), the other chords in the song are F (IV) and G (V). These songs always end on the I chord, and they often start on that same chord too.

The circle of fifths, below, shows you the relationships between the chords. The IV chord is the chord left of the I chord; the V chord is the one right of the I. So if a song ends on C major, it will most probably also use F major (IV) and G major (V).

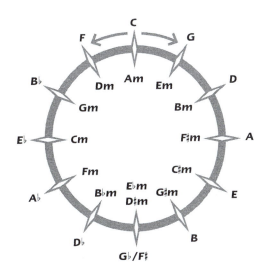

The major chords (C, G, etc.) are on the outside of the circle of fifths. The minor chords (Am, Em, etc.) are on the inside.

Minor

To add a little variation to a song, the I, IV and V chords can be replaced by the corresponding minor chords on the inside of the circle of fifths, for example, replacing C (I) by A minor, and F (IV) by D minor.

223

CHORD PROGRESSIONS

As you can imagine, I, IV, V is not the only popular chord progression. Below are some examples of common progressions in a variety of musical styles. Note that a slash (/) tells you to repeat the preceding chord. Enjoy!

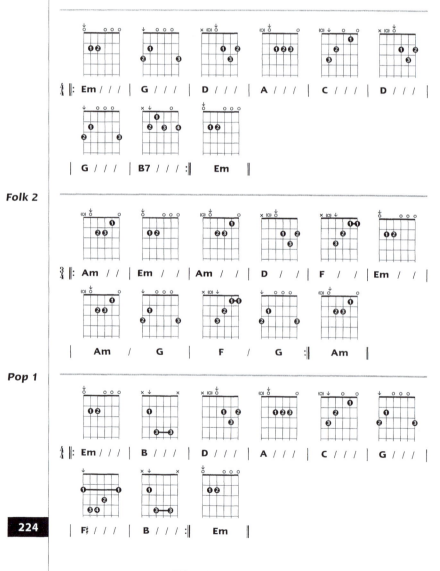

Folk 2

Pop 1

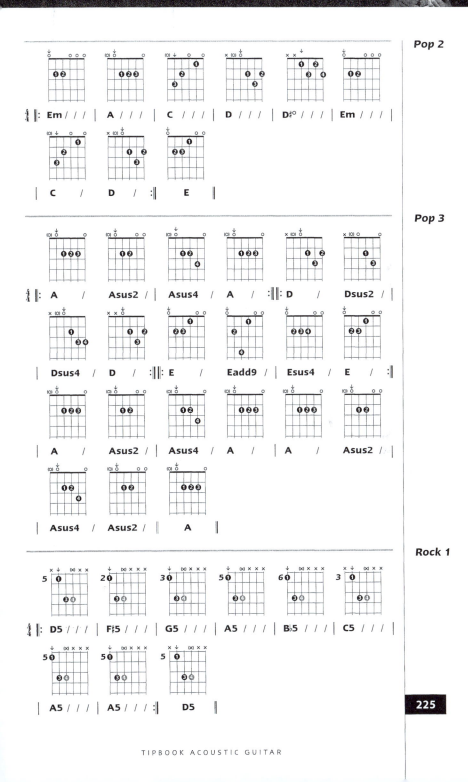

Pop 2

$\frac{4}{4}$ ‖: Em / / / | A / / / | C / / / | D / / / | D♯° / / / | Em / / / |

| C / | D / :‖ E ‖

Pop 3

$\frac{4}{4}$ ‖: A / | Asus2 / | Asus4 / | A / :‖‖: D / | Dsus2 / |

| Dsus4 / | D / :‖‖: E / | Eadd9 / | Esus4 / | E / :‖

| A / | Asus2 / | Asus4 / | A / | A / | Asus2 / |

| Asus4 / | Asus2 / ‖ A ‖

Rock 1

$\frac{4}{4}$ ‖: D5 / / / | F♯5 / / / | G5 / / / | A5 / / / | B♭5 / / / | C5 / / / |

| A5 / / / | A5 / / / :‖ D5 ‖

Rock 2

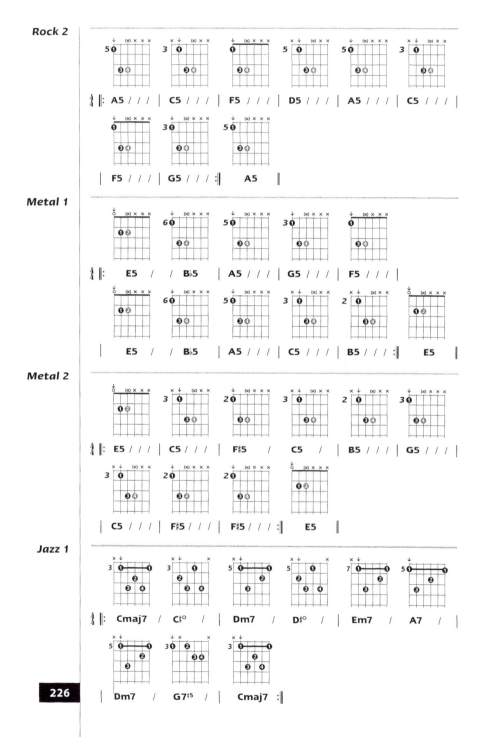

$\frac{4}{4}$ ‖: A5 / / / | C5 / / / | F5 / / / | D5 / / / | A5 / / / | C5 / / / |

| F5 / / / | G5 / / / :‖ A5 ‖

Metal 1

$\frac{4}{4}$ ‖: E5 / / B♭5 | A5 / / / | G5 / / / | F5 / / / |

| E5 / / B♭5 | A5 / / / | C5 / / / | B5 / / / :‖ E5 ‖

Metal 2

$\frac{4}{4}$ ‖: E5 / / / | C5 / / / | F♯5 / | C5 / | B5 / / / | G5 / / / |

| C5 / / / | F♯5 / / / | F♯5 / / / :‖ E5 ‖

Jazz 1

$\frac{4}{4}$ ‖: Cmaj7 / C♯° / | Dm7 / D♯° / | Em7 / A7 / |

| Dm7 / G7♭5 / | Cmaj7 :‖

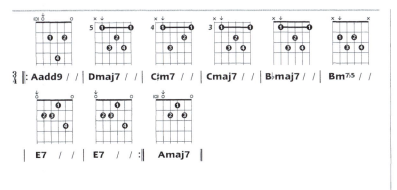

Jazz 2

WEB TIPS

The internet offers many more chords and chord diagrams, and you can also go online to find tabs, lyrics, and anything else you need. Here are some suggestions for informative websites. Enjoy!

- www.looknohands.com/chordhouse
- www.thecipher.com
- www.chordbook.com
- www.guitarchords247.com
- www.e-chords.com
- www.911tabs.com
- www.ultimate-guitar.com
- www.guitaretab.com
- www.mxtabs.net

Essential Data

In the event of your equipment being stolen or lost, or if you decide to sell it, it's useful to have all the relevant data at hand. Here are two pages to make those notes. For the insurance, for the police or just for yourself.

INSURANCE

Company:

Phone: Email:

Agent:

Phone: Email:

Policy no.:   Premium:

INSTRUMENTS AND ACCESSORIES

Make and model:

Serial number: Value:

Specifications:

Date of purchase:

Bought at:

Phone: Email:

Make and model:

Serial number: Value:

Specifications:

Date of purchase:

Bought at:

Phone: Email:

Make and model:

Serial number: Value:

Specifications:

Date of purchase:

Bought at:

Phone: Email:

STRINGS

You're happy with the strings you're using, but somehow you've forgotten what brand, series or gauge they were, or when you put them on...

Make:	Type:	Gauge/Tension:	Date:

Index

Please check out the glossary on pages 171-177 for additional definitions of the terms used in this book.

230

The Tipbook Series

Did you like this Tipbook? There are also Tipbooks for your fellow band or orchestra members! The Tipbook Series features various books on musical instruments, including the singing voice, in addition to Tipbook Music on Paper, Tipbook Amplifiers and Effects, and Tipbook Music for Kids and Teens – a Guide for Parents.

Every Tipbook is a highly accessible and easy-to-read compilation of the knowledge and expertise of numerous musicians, teachers, technicians, and other experts, written for musicians of all ages, at all levels, and in any style of music. Please check www.tipbook.com for up to date information on the Tipbook Series!

All Tipbooks come with Tipcodes that offer additional information, sound files and short movies at www.tipbook. com

Instrument Tipbooks

All instrument Tipbooks offer a wealth of highly accessible, yet well-founded information on one or more closely related instruments. The first chapters of each Tipbook explain the very basics of the instrument(s), explaining all the parts and what they do, describing what's involved in learning to play, and indicating typical instrument prices. The core chapters, addressing advanced players as well, turn you into an instant expert on the instrument. This knowledge allows you to make an informed purchase and get the most out of your instrument. Comprehensive chapters on maintenance, intonation, and tuning are also included, as well a brief section on the history, the family, and the production of the instrument.

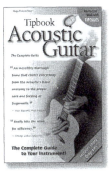

Tipbook Acoustic Guitar – $14.95

Tipbook Acoustic Guitar explains all of the elements that allow you to recognize and judge a guitar's timbre, performance, and playability, focusing on both steel-string and nylon-string instruments. There are chapters covering the various types of strings and their characteristics, and there's plenty of helpful information on changing and cleaning strings, on tuning and maintenance, and even on the care of your fingernails.

233

Tipbook Amplifiers and Effects – $14.95

Whether you need a guitar amp, a sound system, a multi-effects unit for a bass guitar, or a keyboard amplifier, *Tipbook Amplifiers and Effects* helps you to make a good choice. Two chapters explain general features (controls, equalizers, speakers, MIDI, etc.) and figures (watts, ohms, impedance, etc.), and further chapters cover the specifics of guitar amps, bass amps, keyboard amps, acoustic amps, and sound systems. Effects and effect units are dealt with in detail, and there are also chapters on microphones and pickups, and cables and wireless systems.

Tipbook Cello – $14.95

Cellists can find everything they need to know about their instrument in *Tipbook Cello*. The book gives you tips on how to select an instrument and choose a bow, tells you all about the various types of strings and rosins, and gives you helpful tips on the maintenance and tuning of your instrument. Basic information on electric cellos is included as well!

Tipbook Clarinet – $14.95

Tipbook Clarinet sheds light on every element of this fascinating instrument. The knowledge presented in this guide makes trying out and selecting a clarinet much easier, and it turns you into an instant expert on offset and in-line trill keys, rounded or French-style keys, and all other aspects of the instrument. Special chapters are devoted to reeds (selecting, testing, and adjusting reeds), mouthpieces and ligatures, and maintenance.

Tipbook Electric Guitar and Bass Guitar – $14.95

Electric guitars and bass guitars come in many shapes and sizes. *Tipbook Electric Guitar and Bass Guitar* explains all of their features and characteristics, from neck profiles, frets, and types of wood to different types of pickups, tuning machines, and — of course — strings. Tuning and advanced do-it-yourself intonation techniques are included.

Tipbook Drums – $14.95

A drum is a drum is a drum? Not true — and *Tipbook Drums* tells you all the ins and outs of their differences, from the type of wood to the dimensions of the shell, the shape of the bearing edge, and the drum's hardware. Special chapters discuss selecting drum sticks, drum heads, and cymbals. Tuning and muffling, two techniques a drummer must master to make the instrument sound as good as it can, are covered in detail, providing step-by-step instructions.

Tipbook Flute and Piccolo – $14.95

Flute prices range from a few hundred to fifty thousand dollars and more. *Tipbook Flute and Piccolo* tells you how workmanship, materials, and other elements make for different instruments with vastly different prices, and teaches you how to find the instrument that best suits your or your child's needs. Open-hole or closed-hole keys, a B-foot or a C-foot, split-E or donut, inline or offset G? You'll be able to answer all these questions — and more — after reading this guide.

Tipbook Keyboard and Digital Piano – $14.95

Buying a home keyboard or a digital piano may find you confronted with numerous unfamiliar terms. *Tipbook Keyboard and Digital Piano* explains all of them in a very easy-to-read fashion — from hammer action and non-weighted keys to MIDI, layers and splits, arpeggiators and sequencers, expression pedals and multi-switches, and more, including special chapters on how to judge the instrument's sound, accompaniment systems, and the various types of connections these instruments offer.

Tipbook Music for Kids and Teens – a Guide for Parents – $14.95

How do you inspire children to play music? How do you inspire them to practice? What can you do to help them select an instrument, to reduce stage fright, or to practice effectively? What can you do to make practice fun? How do you reduce sound levels and

prevent hearing damage? These and many more questions are dealt with in *Tipbook Music for Kids and Teens – a Guide for Parents and Caregivers*. The book addresses all subjects related to the musical education of children from pre-birth to pre-adulthood.

Tipbook Music on Paper – $14.95

Tipbook Music on Paper – Basic Theory offers everything you need to read and understand the language of music. The book presumes no prior understanding of theory and begins with the basics, explaining standard notation, but moves on to advanced topics such as odd time signatures and transposing music in a fashion that makes things really easy to understand.

Tipbook Piano – $14.95

Choosing a piano becomes a lot easier with the knowledge provided in *Tipbook Piano*, which makes for a better understanding of this complex, expensive instrument without going into too much detail. How to judge and compare piano keyboards and pedals, the influence of the instrument's dimensions, different types of cabinets, how to judge an instrument's timbre, the difference between laminated and solid wood soundboards, accessories, hybrid and digital pianos, and why tuning and regulation are so important: Everything is covered in this handy guide.

Tipbook Saxophone – $14.95

At first glance, all alto saxophones look alike. And all tenor saxophones do too — yet they all play and sound different from each other. *Tipbook Saxophone* discusses the instrument in detail, explaining the key system and the use of additional keys, the different types of pads, corks, and springs, mouthpieces and how they influence timbre and playability, reeds (and how to select and adjust them) and much more. Fingering charts are also included!

Tipbook Trumpet and Trombone, Flugelhorn and Cornet – $14.95

The Tipbook on brass instruments focuses on the smaller horns listed in the title. It explains all of the jargon you come across when you're out to buy or rent an instrument, from bell material to the shape of the bore, the leadpipe, valves and valve slides, and all other elements of the horn. Mouthpieces, a crucial choice for the sound and playability of all brasswinds, are covered in a separate chapter.

Tipbook Violin and Viola – $14.95

Tipbook Violin and Viola covers a wide range of subjects, ranging from an explanation of different types of tuning pegs, fine tuners, and tailpieces, to how body dimensions and the bridge may influence the instrument's timbre. Tips on trying out instruments and bows are included. Special chapters are devoted to the characteristics of different types of strings, bows, and rosins, allowing you to get the most out of your instrument.

Tipbook Vocals – The Singing Voice – $14.95

Tipbook Vocals –The Singing Voice helps you realize the full potential of your singing voice. The book, written in close collaboration with classical and non-classical singers and teachers, allows you to discover the world's most personal and precious instrument without reminding you of anatomy class. Topics include breathing and breath support, singing loudly without hurting your voice, singing in tune, the timbre of your voice, articulation, registers and ranges, memorizing lyrics, and more. The main purpose of the chapter on voice care is to prevent problems.

International editions

The Tipbook Series is also available in Spanish, French, German, Dutch, Italian, Swedish, and Chinese. For more information, please visit us at www.tipbook.com.

Tipbook Series Music and Musical Instruments

Tipbook Acoustic Guitar
ISBN 978-1-4234-4275-2, HL00332373 − $14.95

Tipbook Amplifiers and Effects
ISBN 978-1-4234-6277-4, HL00332776 − $14.95

Tipbook Cello
ISBN 978-1-4234-5623-0, HL00331904 − $14.95

Tipbook Clarinet
ISBN 978-1-4234-6524-9, HL00332803 − $14.95

Tipbook Drums
ISBN 978-90-8767-102-0, HL00331474 − $14.95

Tipbook Electric Guitar and Bass Guitar
ISBN 978-1-4234-4274-5, HL00332372 − $14.95

Tipbook Flute & Piccolo
ISBN 978-1-4234-6525-6, HL00332804 − $14.95

Tipbook Home Keyboard and Digital Piano
ISBN 978-1-4234-4277-6, HL00332375 − $14.95

Tipbook Music for Kids and Teens
ISBN 978-1-4234-6526-3, HL00332805 − $14.95

Tipbook Music on Paper − Basic Theory
ISBN 978-1-4234-6529-4, HL00332807 − $14.95

Tipbook Piano
ISBN 978-1-4234-6278-1, HL00332777 − $14.95

Tipbook Saxophone
ISBN 978-90-8767-101-3, HL00331475 − $14.95

Tipbook Trumpet and Trombone, Flugelhorn and Cornet
ISBN 978-1-4234-6527-0, HL00332806 − $14.95

Tipbook Violin and Viola
ISBN 978-1-4234-4276-9, HL00332374 − $14.95

Tipbook Vocals − The Singing Voice
ISBN 978-1-4234-5622-3, HL00331949 − $14.95

Check www.tipbook.com for additional information!

238